Our Own Selves

More Meditations
for Librarians

MICHAEL GORMAN

Decorations by
Emma Gorman

American Library Association
Chicago   2005

Composition by ALA Editions in Stempel Schneidler.

Printed on 50-pound white offset, a pH-neutral stock, and bound in
10-point coated cover stock by Victor Graphics

The paper used in this publication meets the minimum
requirements of American National Standard for Information
Sciences—Permanence of Paper for Printed Library Materials,
ANSI Z39.48-1992. ∞

Library of Congress Cataloging-in-Publication Data
Gorman, Michael, 1941–
   Our own selves : more meditations for librarians / Michael
     Gorman ; decorations by Emma Gorman.
      p. cm.
   ISBN 0-8389-0896-9 (alk. paper)
   1. Library science—United States. I. Title.
   Z665.2.U6G675 2005
   020'.973—dc22   2004024656

Printed in the United States of America

09 08 07 06 05   5 4 3 2 1

This book is dedicated to

ANNE GORMAN

ANNE REULAND

&

ANNE HEANUE

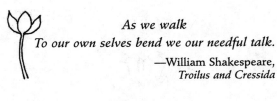
As we walk
To our own selves bend we our needful talk.

—William Shakespeare,
Troilus and Cressida

Contents

Three
People

Four
Values

Five

Library Services

Six

Then and Now

Seven
Technology

Eight
Practicalities

Nine
The Eightfold Path

Ten
This and That

Introduction

I have had the privilege of writing on librarianship and related topics for more than a quarter of a century. I have had
great good fortune in that many of my writings have been
well received, but I have never established the number of
connections with my colleagues (hitherto unknown to me)
that I did with my previous book of meditations—*Our
Singular Strengths*. I hope to be similarly blessed with this
book, and that hope was the main reason for its writing.
My dear friend Art Plotnik, now a full-time polymath and
photographer and then head of ALA Editions, suggested
that first book of meditations and gave me several volumes
in that genre. I disliked them all, finding them vacuous and
unctuous, full of religiosity, and the literary equivalent of
empty calories. However, the idea of short reflections on
many topics accompanied by a quotation and resolution
appealed to me as a literary form. I trust that I have avoided
the smarminess and pomposity all too common in this kind
of thing. I also hope that these thoughts on the many facets
of librarianship establish the kind of connection between
writer and reader that encourages, amuses, and stimulates
thought and reflection. When it does, both writer and
reader gain; though the former may never know of that
gain, he or she is nonetheless enriched. One of the pleasures of writing a book such as this is exploring every possible avenue in search of likely topics. This search can take

one far from the usual professional sources and open up new worlds and new interests, which is always a bracing and salutary experience.

Michael Gorman

Acknowledgments

My heartfelt thanks are due to my friend Anne Heanue, who has read and commented on each of the 100 pieces in this book. Her deep knowledge of the interface between librarianship and society, her keen eye for detail, her willingness to check even the most obscure fact and my wildest fancy, and her capacious memory have provided me with the best gift any writer can receive—a scrupulous reader with a critical intelligence. I am grateful to my assistants, Bernie Griffith and Susan Mangini, for their help and many kindnesses. I am indebted to the many writers (of books, articles, and newspaper columns) and creators of digital content from whom I have taken the germ of an idea leading to one or more of these pieces—some are acknowledged explicitly, most are not. I owe them all a debt. I am also grateful to many of my colleagues at the Madden Library and in the American Library Association who have drawn my attention to an issue or an idea from which I have taken inspiration. I am, as ever, thankful for the encouragement of the staff of ALA Editions, in particular Patrick Hogan, Don Chatham, Marlene Chamberlain, Paul Mendelson, and Dianne Rooney. As age encroaches, the importance of family looms ever larger. I want to thank my brothers and sisters, David, Philippa, Joanna, Timothy, and Paul; my daughters Emma and Alice; their mother, Anne Gorman; and my wife, Anne Reuland, for all the blessings they have given me.

One

Reading
& Books

Head, Heart, and Hand

*Good hearts have made it a warm
and welcoming place.*
—Lawrence Clark Powell

I have just reread a copy of a little pamphlet called *The Three H's*. It was written by, and my copy is signed by, Lawrence Clark Powell. *The Three H's* is the record of a talk given by that polymath and traveler to the Croatian Library Association in 1966. In it, he summons up a vision of a library as a place formed by "good hands" that have made it orderly and efficient; by "good heads" that have not only shaped collections by intelligent choice but have also absorbed a good part of the knowledge contained in those collections; and "good hearts" that exercise service in humility—motivated by a love of people and learning. It is interesting to note that the criteria for the John Muir Award, given to those who exemplify the ideas of the great naturalist, are based on the same model. To the John Muir Trust, the head equals understanding, the hand doing, and the heart caring.

Powell's is a concept of library work that would not have seemed strange to a librarian of 1866 but may to a librarian of 2005. A scant third of a century after Powell wrote his pamphlet, his vision of learning, of the tactile pleasures of books and reading, and the joys of library service is a reminder of what we may be losing. It is hard to see good hands, heads, and hearts in some manifestations of the modern library, and the pleasures of handling and reading books are remote from the chilly allure of the screen and the keyboard. Be that as it may, libraries are about service or they are about nothing, and

the hands, heads, and hearts of modern librarians are well employed when they are engaged in delivering that service—by whichever means are the best for library users.

I will use my head and heart together
to inform the work of my hands.

The Fragile Human Record

*This world where much is to be done
and little to be known.*

—Samuel Johnson

If I were asked to recommend one book on modern libraries it would be a somewhat paradoxical choice—Lionel Casson's *Libraries in the Ancient World* (2001). This is a book well worth reading on its own merits—concision, narrative power, and scholarship—but to the modern librarian with a taste for speculation, it is the parallels to, and antecedents of, our own work that are most fascinating. Casson tells us that the first libraries were those of the Sumerians, in the middle of the third millennium BCE, but the Egyptians were not far behind. We know far more about the Sumerians and their libraries simply because of the medium they used—clay tablets—whereas the Egyptians used papyrus. The former is actually rendered more durable by fire, whereas the latter is highly flammable. In Casson's words "They [Egyptian libraries] existed, to be sure, but we know of them only vaguely and indirectly." The medium may not be the message, but it certainly has a dramatic effect on the transmission of the message to future generations.

This is worth pondering in our time, when communication may well be dominated by a medium that makes papyrus look like carved stone by comparison. Casson's book has a sad subtext. It is replete with phrases like "we will never know," "has not survived," and "too few codices from the relevant centuries have survived." Only a minute fraction of Greek literature is still extant, and Latin and other ancient texts have fared no

better. We have also much to learn from the early days of the manuscript age, which lasted for 1,000 years after the end of the Roman Empire. None of these lessons is more important than the fact that the onward transmission of the human record is imperiled when that record is made in unique copies and in a perishable medium. We like to believe in progress, but the truth is that the electronic age may be just a rerun of the manuscript age, and the print age may come to be seen as a 500-year aberration—an island of fixity in an ocean of loss.

I will value the records of humankind
and work to preserve them.

Word Pictures

Melting, melodious words, to lutes of amber.
—Robert Herrick

I learned to read at so young an age that I have no memory of not being able to read. I have vivid memories of reading when less than four years old, but none at all of puzzling out words or trying to decipher characters on the page. I must have gone through those latter processes, but I grew up feeling that reading was as natural and as easily acquired a skill as walking. Perhaps that is the reason why words not only convey but also depict their meanings to my eyes. I have read very widely about reading, but have never come across a reference to this peculiarity. For example, in that last sentence, the word "widely" looks, well, wide; and there is something about the first half of "peculiarity" that has a strangeness and singularity to my eyes as if the word were grimacing at me. It is a difficult thing to write about. When reading, I just accept this other pictorial layer of meaning and the richness it adds to the reading experience—except perhaps when reading poetry, in which meaning and image are inextricably linked and the look of the words heightens the images they evoke. While writing, I am always in danger of entering a verbal hall of mirrors—a place of unbearable self-consciousness in which words like "vivid," "easily," "difficult," and "richness" (all used in this paragraph) leap off the page and dance in the air (just as the word "dance" looks lively and vivacious—but this way lies madness!).

I will always enjoy the richness of language
in the love of reading.

Choice of Reading

In conversing with Books we may chuse
our Company, and disengage without
Ceremony or Exception. Here we are free
from the Formalities of Custom and Respect:
we need not undergo the Penance of a Dull
Story . . . but may shake off
the Haughty, the Impertinent, and
the Vain, at Pleasure.

—Jeremy Collier,
Essays on Several Moral Subjects

Collier was quite right, of course. If the book you are reading is not to your liking at the time, put it aside and come back to it sometime or never. (Dorothy Parker's legend has it that her review of one book consisted of "This is not a book to be lightly put aside. It is a book to be hurled across the room.") If you love the book you are reading, you may put it aside for a while just to prolong the time before you reach its end. If you find you have borrowed a Dull Story from the library, return it and go in search of books that are neither haughty nor impertinent nor vain. In the mid-twentieth century, futurists predicted that robots would be doing our household chores by now (while we commuted to work in personal helicopters and on moving sidewalks). Just like the robots, a book is there, patient and untiring, twenty-four hours a day, every day of every year, waiting to be brought to life by inquiring eyes and minds.

I recently gave a small collection of books to the Arne Nixon Center for the Study of Children's Literature (the jewel

in my library's crown). They were examples of an all but forgotten genre—the historical adventure story for boys pioneered by the likes of G. A. Henty and R. M. Ballantyne in the nineteenth century. I read them and many others in great numbers when in my teens. To tell the truth, what little I know of history was gained from, and inspired by, such books. Today it is the colored illustrated book covers that make them of interest rather than the didactic text and wooden dialogue. Those books had accompanied me from England to Illinois and from thence to California. Before I assembled them for transportation to the library, I opened each of them one Sunday afternoon and read passages from each—for the first time in more than fifty years. My friends were still there, the black-hearted villains still villainous, the heroes (often no more than boys themselves) still clean-cut and fearless. They were just waiting to be brought alive by the opening of the book, just as they will wait in silence for their next reader.

I will remember that books have riches
that never tarnish or fade.

Another "Virtual Library"

*Read the most useful books and that
regularly, and constantly. Steadily spend all
the morning in this employ or, at least
five hours in four and twenty.*

—John Wesley, *Minutes of
Some Late Conversations*

You've come to a friendly place, and we welcome you to
our book-lovers' community. What is BookCrossing, you
ask? It's a global book club that crosses time and space. It's
a reading group that knows no geographical boundaries.
Do you like free books? How about free book clubs? Well,
the books our members leave in the wild are free . . . but it's
the act of freeing books that points to the heart of Book-
Crossing. Book trading has never been more exciting, more
serendipitous, than with BookCrossing. Our goal, simply, is
to make the whole world a library. BookCrossing is a book
exchange of infinite proportion, the first and only of its kind.

This is the credo of an interesting group called BookCrossing
that maintains a website called www.bookcrossing.com that
is central to its activities. The group was founded in early 2001
and has a simple purpose—to spread the reading and discussion of books throughout the United States. Their method is
to leave books, once read by a member and entered on the
website, in such places as cafes, train stations, airports, parks,
and coffee shops. The books are labeled as being from a
member of the group and give the website address with an in-
vitation to read the book and to add the reader's impressions

to the dialogue on the site. The jargon of the group includes "releasing the books into the wild" and the books being "caught" when they are found and read. The idea has spread to more than 80 countries and the group has more than 70,000 members—each registering and releasing books into the wild after they are read.

So the Amazon.com Paradox finds another voice. The use of electronic technology to assist in the creation of a global reading group and a free book club is almost as astonishing as Amazon.com itself, based solidly on the selling of real books (not e-books) and one of the few successful purely e-commercial enterprises.

There is a pleasantly anarchic aspect to the BookCrossing enterprise. The anarchic nature is reinforced by the randomness implicit in whether the released books are found or not and, if found, whether they will be read or not and, if read, whether the reader will post her or his responses to the website. About one in four of the books released into the wild are "caught"—that is, found, read, and recorded on the website—which is a very high ratio when one thinks of the perils awaiting a book left in a public place. The fact is that all such enterprises are good in that they spread the opportunity to read and the opportunity to share the reading experience with others. This "virtual library" is no challenge to real libraries but a complementary effort that creates better-read people and a climate of learning and communication from chance encounters.

*I will encourage all efforts that lead
to more reading.*

Living with Bibliomania

Five hundred times at least, I've said—
My wife assures me—"I would never
Buy more old books"; yet lists are made
And shelves are lumbered more than ever.

—Anonymous

I once had the great pleasure of hearing a longtime friend give two lectures on the pleasures and travails of book collecting. Jack Walsdorf is a man of parts. He is a librarian, a bookseller, a bibliographer, a bibliophile, and an author. His fifteen books on bookmaking and bibliography include several on William Morris and the Kelmscott Press, on both of which he is an internationally recognized expert. He brought all of this background and experience to bear in those two presentations. The first lecture was a highly entertaining mixture of reminiscence and practical advice for those wishing to follow him down the primrose path of bibliomania, without succumbing to its worst excesses. His many stories of the effects of careful searching for desired volumes balanced with serendipitous discovery were both enjoyable and instructive. His principal injunctions were to live within a book-buying budget and to focus on an area of specialization. Both are of great value to the book collector and are greatly in danger of being ignored by the hardcore bibliomaniac. In my experience, there is always money for another book, no matter the state of even the most elastic budget, and there is always a book *just* (or even, to be truthful, far) outside your area of focus that simply cries out to be acquired. The book collector who lives within her or his means

and sticks to books in the exact area of collection is like a colleague with an immaculately neat desk, a stamp collector with every stamp hinged to its correct page or filed in little glassine envelopes in perfect order, or a dieter who never breaks a diet—admirable, rare, and more than slightly annoying.

The second lecture was on the "ABCs of Book Collecting"—more rules aimed at keeping bibliomania in check and the basis for expert disquisitions on matters as varied as Victorian book illustration, decorated bindings, marbled endpapers, the condition of original dust jackets, the added value of volumes signed (and even better, inscribed) by their authors, the relative value of first and variant editions, and all the other arcana of book collecting. The ineffable sadness of the mundane was found in his accurate if depressing observation that the price one would pay a bookseller for a book is, almost invariably, *three times* what that bookseller would pay you for the same volume. Jack's talks told me that rules are made to be lived with, not obeyed, and that the highs of bibliomania are as high, and the lows are as low, as the ups and downs of more earthly loves.

**I will love books almost as much
as I love people.**

Alone and Never Alone

*I love the solitude of reading. I love
the deep dive into someone else's story,
the delicious ache of a last page. I love the
wide basket in which shining fruits rest
together on a table. The sense of gathering,
the gleam, seems similar to the bounty
offered by an anthology.*

—Naomi Shihab Nye,
Books Change Lives

Unless one is participating in the millennia-old ceremony of a reading or storytelling, the act of interacting with the stories of others is done alone. The iconic picture of a reader is of one in a quiet unpeopled room or in an isolated island of light in the quiet reading room of a library. The stereotypical "ssshh-ing" of a librarian is a sign of the desire to preserve that quiet, that solitude, for those reading even in a busy library. Library design, library furniture, and library lighting have all centered on the idea of providing privacy and quiet to those studying. Though few have gone so far as Marcel Proust, who created a cork-lined room in his house to guarantee absolute silence, we all have a notion, perhaps a dream, of a special quiet place in which to read. The paradox is that this thirst for quiet and aloneness arises from a desire to provide a way for us to never be alone. We wish for solitude in order to enter worlds teeming with people, events, and ideas. In a library, we wish to shut out all the other people in the building so that we can commune with all the people in the buildings in our minds.

14

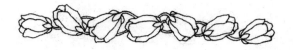

This is completely different from the solitude of meditation, the search for selflessness (going beyond the self) that is characteristic of Eastern meditation. We seek the solitude of reading to realize the self, not to abandon it. That realization of self is through the "deep dive into somebody else's story" of which Naomi Nye writes. The metaphor of the diver silent on the springboard expresses the silence we seek before we open a book, that moment of stillness before we immerse ourselves in other worlds. That immersion is far easier for children, even in the absence of silence, but it is available to us all, given the right conditions, and can be a blessing throughout the longest of lives.

I will appreciate the solitude of reading.

Living Things

For books are not absolutely dead things,
but they do contain a potency of life in them
to be as active as that soul whose progeny
they are; nay, they do preserve as in a vial
the purest efficacy and extraction of that
living intellect that bred them.

—John Milton, *Areopagitica*

John Milton wrote his *Areopagitica* as an attack on what we would now call "prior restraint" on the part of the Roundhead government of Oliver Cromwell, which was busy restoring the system of licensing and censorship that had been one of the reasons they overthrew the tyranny of King Charles I and his Star Chamber. This is, alas, a not unfamiliar pattern. The French revolutionaries overthrew the despotic monarchs and within a few years were as despotic themselves, the Soviet revolution against the brutalities of the czars resulted in greater brutalities, and the level of repression in China has not varied much through the reigns of the emperors, the Kuomintang, and the Communists. The sharp bright sword of idealism brings about revolutions but is soon blunted by the exercise of power. The rhetoric changes but the urge to repress and censor is undying. The world has generally made progress, but the government's reaction to the unspeakable events of September 11, 2001, should remind us that the urge to sacrifice freedom for "security" (as defined by the powerful) lies unsleeping if, in the modern world, mostly restrained.

For Milton, freedom and truth were the most important things of the life of the mind. (Though it should be noted that he, a seventeenth-century English Protestant, understood truth to be religious truth and freedom not extending to papists and infidels.) Milton also believed that truth would always prevail in the long run—though to the modern eye, that run is sometimes very long indeed. That is why freedom mattered so much to him. He thought that all should have a voice and be able to publish what they wish (though by "all" he meant all Protestants and anti-royalists) because truth would win and error would fail in the clash of ideas that arises from the freedom of the presses. His opposition to the prior censorship of his (anti-royalist) side was as absolute as his opposition to the censorship of King Charles and the royalists. The most important thing about that opposition was his understanding of the power of books and the way in which they preserve the distilled essence of their authors. To him, and to generations that followed him, the intense power of the printed word and the reason why it should be unfettered came from precisely this understanding of a book as a living thing—the ideas and soul of its author preserved in the "vial" of a codex. To Milton, the act of reading is an act of communing with another mind, and that communion should be free of all restraints in order that the truth should be known.

*I will cherish the living
nature of books.*

The Power of Children's Books

> *The glamour*
> *Of childish days is upon me,*
> *my manhood is cast*
> *Down in the flood of remembrance,*
> *I weep like a child for the past.*
>
> —D. H. Lawrence, *Piano*

When asked which book had made him want to be a writer, Tom Wolfe wrote an elegant essay on how there are certain books in every writer's life that ignite the desire to write in a life-changing way. He cited, among others, Steinbeck, James M. Cain, Waugh, Mencken, Thomas Wolfe, Gay Talese, Céline, and Henry Miller as great influences on his style and the way in which he matured as a writer. For the book that "galvanized" him and made him decide to be a writer, however, Wolfe turned to an entirely different writer in a different genre. That book was *Honey Bear* by Dixie Willson, illustrated by Maginel Wright Barney, published in the early 1920s. Wolfe learnedly describes the text as "rollicking and rolling rhythm: anapestic quadrameter with spondees at regular intervals." Fortunately for the rest of us who cannot grasp what this might be, he gives examples, and rollicking they are, too.

> *Once upon a summer in the hills by the river*
>
> *Was a deep green forest where the wild things grew.*
>
> *There were caves as dark as midnight—there were tangled*
> *trees and thickets*
>
> *And a thousand little places where the sky looked through.*

It is easy to see how the infant Wolfe was captivated by the rhythms, rhymes, and wordplay of such a book and how, even in the days before he could read, he decided that he wanted to be a writer. He says that *Honey Bear* made him think that writing could be magic and fun, and he, "lying illiterate on my little pillow in a tiny bed," resolved then and there to be a writer. He adds, wryly, that writing mostly turned out to be not magic and fun, but the die was cast when he was captivated by his mother's readings long ago.

What is it about a good children's book that has such a seismic effect on so many lives? What is the special magic of children's books that we remember all our lives and that is more intense than even the most profound reading experience as an adult? I think it is that those early books are the first that transport us out of the egocentric life of the child, conjuring worlds of experience and events about which we had never dreamed. Although that magic transcends the self-centeredness of the child, it also allows that self to roam and become part of the story and the magic. We adults can read and enjoy the Harry Potter books, but there are millions of children who read and participate in the stories, not just imagining themselves in but also *living* in Hogwarts School.

> *I will always be aware of the power*
> *of children's books.*

Four Centuries
of Information Overload

A confusing and harmful abundance of books.
—Conrad Gesner

As in every age, we tend to think our problems are unique because we believe that the circumstances in which we live are unique. There has never been such a revolution as that being wrought by technology, we tell ourselves, and no one in human history has lived through a period of such stress and strain. We talk of burnout (as if no one before us had known despair), of the stress of modern life (as if the daily life of a medieval peasant were all carefree cakes and ale), and, in our profession, of information overload. It turns out that the latter uniquely modern evil is neither unique nor uniquely modern. The Harvard intellectual historian Ann Blair has documented the many ways in which scholars in the sixteenth through eighteenth centuries attempted to deal with the information overload caused by the multiplicity of books being published. Conrad Gesner's complaint at the head of this essay was made in the preface to his *Bibliotheca universalis*—an attempt to catalogue all known books—published in 1545, a scant century after Gutenberg introduced printing to the West and the modern book was born. Professor Blair tells us of the gloomy prognostications of Adrien Baillet in 1685. He believed that the sheer numbers of books then available would cause a new age of barbarism that would be as bad as the Dark Ages after the fall of the Roman Empire, because society would be unable to absorb all the knowledge and information those books contained.

The first reaction to this crisis of information overload was the near-universal call for discrimination in reading. Scholars were abjured to read only the best books and not to clutter their minds with lesser publications. There is more than an echo of that in the advice given to web users today to seek out the small amount of electronic wheat in the mountains of electronic chaff. In 1614 Father Francesco Sacchini, S.J., told young men not to read new books but rather reread those "good" books chosen by teachers. There were many other responses to the existential panic induced in those long-ago readers by the proliferation of books. They included levels of reading—skimming the majority of books (an ancient kind of surfing) and reading only "good" books carefully; the introduction of indexes, tables of contents, etc., to allow the reader to read only selected parts of new books; and the production of encyclopedias and other compendia that substituted one book for a multitude. Just as we know today that the number of "worthwhile" electronic documents is smaller than the number of the other kind and are trying to devise schemes to find the former and avoid the latter, the scholars of centuries ago knew that, as John Ruskin put it in the nineteenth century, "All books are divisible into two classes, the books of the hour and the books of all time."

*I will seek the valuable and
enduring in all my reading.*

Two

Places

The Quincy Library Group

A green thought in a green shade.
—Andrew Marvell, *The Garden*

The headquarters of the Plumas County Library is situated in Quincy, California, a town of some 1,300 souls near the Feather River in the inland north of the state. The three-county area (Plumas together with adjacent Lassen and Sierra counties) is about the size of Austria. The counties mainly consist of federally owned coniferous forests and thus are heavily dependent on the logging industry. The area is Ground Zero of the "timber wars"—bitter multilateral battles between environmentalists, logging companies, local residents, and the federal government. Most notoriously, the great issue and symbol of the "war" is the California spotted owl—an endangered bird taken as a harbinger of eco-crisis to come by one side and as a destroyer of jobs by the other.

There is at least one group that has worked to reconcile the various parties in the timber wars and to develop detailed plans that would meet acceptance by the community and governments (federal, state, and local), protect endangered species, promote forest health, and create harmony out of conflict. This group—the Quincy Library Group—arose out of discussions between a timber industry representative, a local government official, and an environmental lawyer in 1992. Those discussions took place in the county library in Quincy and the group, now thirty members strong, has held many meetings there in the thirteen years since. The one-story, blue-roofed building surrounded by tall conifers is not the only public place in Quincy or the other small towns in the

three counties—Susanville, Sierra City, Calpine—but it cannot be bettered symbolically. What better place for adversaries to come together to resolve their issues and problems than the county library headquarters—the intellectual and cultural heart of this green and beautiful region?

I will always remember
the central role
of the public library
in the community.

Old Library, New Museum

*Washington combines Northern charm
and Southern efficiency.*
—John F. Kennedy

In May 2003, the once-abandoned Carnegie Library in downtown Washington, D.C., opened as the City Museum, telling the story of real life and real people in what seems at times to be the most unreal of cities. The Historical Society of Washington operates the museum. The District of Columbia, carved out of the state of Maryland to be the center of the American democratic ideal, is, among its other curiosities, a profoundly undemocratic place. Its citizens elect no senators or representatives, and the people they do elect at the local level have powers that are severely restricted by the members of Congress they played no part in electing. Another singularity is that the District of Columbia is the political capital of the United States, but not the capital in any other sense. It is a one-industry town and that industry—government—is not leavened by the influence of any other industry. In Europe, the capitals dominate in terms of government, finance, the arts and entertainment, sport, etc. In the United States, New York, Los Angeles, and Chicago are all "capitals" of one or another aspect of American collective life. This means that, in the popular mind, Washington equals "government" and little else and its history is perceived as similarly one-dimensional. There is, however, a real and rich story to tell that takes the visitor past the symbols of government and power and past the monumental, iconic facade of the "world's largest village."

One aspect of that story lies in the historic building that now houses the Washington City Museum. The Beaux Arts building was once the city's first public library, built on Mount Vernon Square in 1903. It closed in 1972, when the Martin Luther King, Jr., Memorial Library building was opened. It was abandoned until taken over by the University of the District of Columbia in the 1980s. The building has been painstakingly restored at a cost of more than $20 million. More significantly than any of this, the library was one of the very few public buildings in Washington that was never segregated. How fitting that the library should have been a place of service to all throughout the long years of the twentieth century in which discrimination wore a public face and bigotry was a stain on this country and its capital city.

I will be aware of the history
of my library in its community.

The Library Hotel

A whiskered cove who looked like a bandit, as no doubt he was, being the proprietor of the hotel.

—P. G. Wodehouse,
Aunt Agatha Takes the Count

Perhaps the Dewey decimal classification (DDC) system is so deep in the American psyche that many think it a natural phenomenon. Perhaps the general populace believes that the Dewey classification was written so long ago that it is like the Law of the Medes and Persians, the Ten Commandments, or the periodic table of elements, and therefore an immutable and public part of the general culture. Perhaps most people do not know that Melvil Dewey was a real person and not a mythic figure like Johnny Appleseed or Paul Bunyan. Perhaps few people who know that Dewey did exist could distinguish between John and Melvil and Admiral Dewey. Perhaps there are large numbers of people who think that Dewey is one of a trio of cartoon ducks. However it may be, knowledge that the Dewey system is not only the product of a single mind but also an ever-changing and evolving commodity of great value to its owners is restricted to librarians and not even to all librarians at that. Even library users seldom bother to think about those numbers that disfigure the spines of library books, pausing only to be irritated by the iron law that makes the shortest numbers applicable to the biggest books and the longest numbers to the slimmest pamphlets.

Given the general ignorance of the origins, nature, ownership, and use of the world's most popular classification system,

it is hardly surprising that the owners of a luxury hotel (opened in 2000) within sight and sound of the lions of the New York Public Library headquarters should feel free to call it the Library Hotel, number its floors after the ten main classes of the DDC, and assign specific DDC numbers to its rooms. For example, one room is numbered 700.003 (performing arts) and contains, along with the usual hotel furniture, books on the theatre, opera, ballet, etc. George Bernard Shaw wrote, "The great advantage of a hotel is that it is a refuge from family life." Unless the guest at the Library Hotel were a librarian in the habit of labeling parts of her home with DDC numbers (a type not commonly found in the luxury hotels of New York), this would truly be different from home life and all innocent fun.

Not so, said OCLC, which, it turns out, is the owner of the Dewey decimal classification and all its trademarked features. Lawyers have stated that OCLC has a good case, but it is hard for those of us not of that learned profession to see what possible harm can accrue to OCLC by this unorthodox use of DDC numbers. The case is unsettled as I write and perhaps OCLC, twirling its moustaches and laughing villainously, will succeed in bankrupting the Library Hotel and preserving the pristine virtue of DDC numbers. I hope not. I had a colleague many years ago who would send picture postcards from holiday locations all written in DDC numbers (the name of the place, rain, beaches, horse-riding, palms, etc.). He is dead now and perhaps that is just as well, because OCLC would have him up in front of a judge if they ever learned of his copyright-breaking postcards.

I will try to apply common sense to everyday situations.

Frank's Library

Bright the vision that delighted.
—Richard Mant,
Ancient Hymns

One of my colleagues has a fourteen-year-old son called Frank. He is an intelligent and bookish young man who does exceptionally well at school and seems to have a glittering academic career ahead of him. One unusual thing about him is that he has the aspiration to become, by means not yet decided, an eccentric billionaire. Would that we all had such lofty and interesting goals. One of his projects, when he has achieved billionairedom, is to create and run what he modestly calls "the world's biggest library." Some of the features of Frank's library offer a user's perspective that is both provocative and unusual. For example, a planning detail that does not show up in most texts on library planning is the idea of having carpeting in the aisles between the stacks. The idea behind this is that a browser could, on finding the right reading material, simply lie on the floor in comfort and read the book right there and then. Another, more traditional detail, if one with a twist, is that his library will have many rooms on many stories, each with shelves and volumes, so that the users, even if there were many of them at one time, could be guaranteed quiet and a degree of privacy. The central room will have tables and chairs for working but also fireplaces with armchairs and couches for comfortable reading. The prime division of the library will be between pleasure reading and research, with the materials that have something of each in an indeterminate zone between.

Frank is not enamored of technology except as a support for the central activity of reading, but he has one interesting technological suggestion. He would have each book tagged with a device that would send its exact location to a central monitor. If, at the end of the day, a book has been left out on a table or was misshelved, the device would send a notification to ensure the book is returned to its proper spot. Frank, a modernist, is not particularly interested in rare volumes of interest to the few, but wants the collections to have many copies of the most popular titles. Sliding ladders giving access (to the nimble) to high shelves will be another feature of the library. A special alcove, known to and accessible to Frank only, will lie at the top of the tallest of the ladders. There he could keep and read his favorite books and from there he could survey the main reading areas and watch the beneficiaries of his philanthropy enjoy its fruits. This may smack of elitism, but what is the point of being a generous eccentric billionaire if there are no extras in life? The central design theme of the library will be curving lines (Frank believes the rectilinear nature of most library materials calls to be offset by fluid shapes), so one can imagine a place of mystery in which each curving path leads to round and elliptical reading areas adjacent to gently curving shelves—another innovation in library design. Additionally, he would like few, if any, windows in the library, as vistas are too distracting. His mother, a museologist, told him of the theory that after concentrating on a single object, one needs vistas to prevent "museum fatigue." In Frank's opinion, that might be fine in museums, but in libraries the books are all the vistas you need.

I will persist in my vision
of what libraries can be.

The School Library

*Mrs. Ryll's library was the one constant
through my high school years. I changed
teachers and classrooms. I changed social
groups. I changed personalities and clothing
styles and political beliefs over the course
of those years. The library was like the friend
who embraced all your different
incarnations, happily following your interest
in Buddhism or muscle cars, but was
always the same old friend.*

—Joan Ryan, in
the *San Francisco Chronicle*

Sadly, Joan Ryan's happy memories of an island of stability in her teen years were prompted by the decision of a large northern California school district in 2004 to cut all high school sports, eliminate all music teachers and counselors, and close down all its libraries. It is hardly surprising that this decision provoked great outrage and vociferous protests . . . about the elimination of high school sports. School sports occupy such a hallowed place in the schools and communities of America that a cynic might wonder if the expressed desire to eliminate them from the West Contra Costa District was an alarmist threat that, if not carried out, would lead to such relief that the libraries and music programs could be assassinated with impunity. (No government entity would act in such a Machiavellian manner, of course.)

Various banks and sports teams have chipped into a fund for the school district, motivated, one imagines, by the threat to sports rather than those to music and libraries. As Ryan points out, however, these one-time charitable donations to public services are no substitute for consistent, continuing monetary support of the type that can only be provided by public funding. It is one thing to buy the equipment for a baseball team, the instruments for a school band, and some books for a school library's shelves. It is quite another to fund, over many years, a baseball coach, a music teacher, or a school librarian and to provide a steady stream of the best literature for children and young adults. I know that young people need sports and music and their lives are impoverished in the absence of either, but I think depriving them of good school library service is a far greater impoverishment. It is a deprivation, as Joan Ryan writes, of a constant friendly presence, a place in which the lonely and the introverted can be themselves and grow. In a library, young misfits are equal to the athletes and socially gifted. A good school library and a good school librarian will welcome all the many kinds of young persons and will give them services that enrich and comfort in equal measure.

> *I will always support school libraries*
> *and school librarians.*

Trains and Boats and Planes

My boat sails freely,
both with wind and stream.
—William Shakespeare,
Othello

Libraries have reached out to those who cannot visit them, for one reason or another, for more than a century. A friend of mine once participated in a public library service that delivered books to the incarcerated in a notorious London prison. He made many interesting acquaintances thereby. Even urban libraries have services that deliver to the housebound and the hospitalized, but our dominant image of such reaching out is the motorized mobile library that serves rural communities and individuals. This kind of mobile library is the norm in most of North America and western Europe, but mobile services take other forms in other parts of the world and even in the remoter parts of this continent and Europe.

The good people of the Prince Rupert Public Library in British Columbia have assembled a list of mobile libraries worldwide following the launch of their own book boats in 2000. This list of "unusual libraries" includes boat libraries in Norway, Sweden, Alaska, Florida (in Boca Grande until 1964), Argentina, and Thailand. Each tells the story of a practical adaptation to local circumstances, of boats laden with books traveling rivers, fjords, and the channels between islands to deliver services to people living in otherwise inaccessible places, and of people in our profession using unconventional means to achieve our ideals. In Nunavut, Canada's vast and sparsely populated northern territory (two million square kilo-

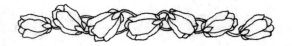

meters with 29,000 inhabitants), librarians use both dogsleds and snowmobiles to deliver library services. In Copiapó, Chile, the inhabitants circulate eight "magical trunks of books" to senior centers in the community, each accompanied by a librarian to act as a reader's advisor. In Nkayi, Zimbabwe, there are four donkey-drawn traveling libraries, each equipped with solar-powered communication units that power video players, etc., as well as book collections. There are six camel-drawn traveling libraries in northeastern Kenya, serving a population of more than a million. The Prince Rupert Library documents book trains in Bangkok, bicycle book-delivery services and backpack libraries in Chile, and libraries on mission boats in various parts of the world, including British Columbia. The U.S. Navy boasts of its many libraries aboard aircraft carriers and other vessels. There are libraries on commuter buses in Thailand. I could not find any aircraft libraries, but I wonder if Australia might have had such a service and Flying Librarians to go with its Flying Doctors? The point is that librarians everywhere will seek out every way possible of providing library services to all, and we should be proud of our endless adaptability and inventiveness.

I will value the unorthodox
in library service.

Ancient and Modern

Architecture in general is frozen music.

—Friedrich von Schelling,
Philosophy of Art

Library buildings have fascinated me since I was a young child. My early memories are of imposing stone edifices in a vaguely Gothic or classical style (the central public libraries) or of nondescript brick buildings absolutely lacking in artifice (the neighborhood branches). Long ago, college and university libraries of any size came in academic Gothic or, in this country, Midwestern neoclassical. The library in my first school was in a prefabricated structure, just a step or two above a shed. I am writing this in a soon-to-be demolished library that I have compared unfavorably to a Bulgarian police station, such is its almost total charmlessness. Because this library is to be demolished and a new building erected on its site, I have been taking a keen interest in recent developments in library architecture.

There seem to be two dominant themes in modern library architecture. The first is the idea of integrating with, and building on, the past in the form of adding to, renovating, and adapting existing structures, which may or may not have been libraries before. From such projects that I have seen, or of which I have seen pictures, the meld of ancient and modern is sometimes brilliant, sometimes seamless, and sometimes awkward. Sometimes an architect of taste will not even attempt seamlessness and will create an additional structure with different materials that nevertheless harmonizes perfectly

with the existing building. Sometimes such attempts make you wince.

The second dominant trend lies in the use of light. Thomas Fuller wrote (in 1642): "Light (God's eldest daughter) is a principal beauty in building." However theologically unsound that may be, it is certainly true that light is a major element in the frozen music that is architecture. Large libraries used to be dark places lit by low artificial light in most rooms, echoing, as in many other features, ancient church architecture. The metaphor of the library as temple of learning was taken seriously and great soaring, vaulted roofs and high windows were the result, as were shafts of dusty light beaming down on the library's ark of the covenant—the card catalogue. Not so with the new and renovated library buildings of the early twenty-first century. Light abounds in these structures, many of which are airy visions in glass and steel.

The wide variation in styles that results from the combination of integration and renovation with the new ethic of light is another thing that fascinates me. Libraries that are modernist and neomodernist are to be seen in the pages of architectural magazines beside neoclassical renovated warehouses, Prairie School libraries nestling into their environment, and all manner of others in a multitude of shapes, sizes, materials, and effects. We live in an age of experimentation and diversity in library building that will resonate for decades to come.

I will appreciate the beauty and usefulness
of library buildings—new and old.

The Southern California Library

Talk California—a state so blessed
He said, in climate, no one had ever died there
A natural death.

—Robert Frost, *New Hampshire*

I have lived in California—that state so blessed and cursed—
for more than fifteen years, which is the longest time I have
ever lived anywhere except my native Britain. It is a state of
contrasts and contradictions and of regions that are as unlike
each other—politically, geographically, socially, and every
which way—as, say, Delaware and New Mexico. The Inland
Empire east of Los Angeles and the vast area from San
Francisco north to the Oregon border could not be more different if they were different states. Most people who do not
live here still think that California is made up of Southern
California and the Bay Area, the coastal homes of the great
cities of the Golden State, and forget, or know nothing of, the
great Central Valley, the deserts, and the ecotopia of the
North. This is sad because no matter how potent the Southern
California dreamin' of the Beach Boys and the lingering image
of the city in which Tony Bennett left his heart and the cable
cars climbing to the stars may be, there is far more to the reality
of California than sun and surf and goofy elected officials.

The political life of California is documented in its many
great libraries, and in them we can discover that life is far
deeper and more nuanced than most outsiders can imagine.
For example, the fabled city of Los Angeles is much more than
the La-La Land myth. Its labor and progressive history are doc-

umented in the Southern California Library for Social Studies and Research (SCL). Emil Freed and his wife Tassia founded this nonprofit special library in the 1960s. It contains thousands of books and other library materials on the labor movement, the women's movement, civil liberties, people of color, left-wing culture, peace, radicalism, socialism, and other causes in Los Angeles and the rest of Southern California. It is a major archive for materials on social change focusing on Los Angeles, including pamphlets, posters, photos, films, videos, audiotapes, subject files, organizational records, personal papers, and more. Its funding comes from individuals and some grants.

The SCL lives up to the highest aspirations of librarianship by collecting and preserving the record of social justice movements in the area; by connecting those collections to contemporary issues such as peace, civil liberties, racial profiling, the living wage, and affordable housing; by serving as a gathering place for people interested in social change in Los Angeles; and by celebrating their heritage through films, music, and more. The point of this is not to praise the SCL or even the eminently praiseworthy Golden State, but to cite the SCL as an example of the thousands of libraries—special, public, and academic—that pursue an ideal not only by preserving and making available a wide range of materials in their subject areas, but also by acting as the center of the community they serve and as the place in which the aspirations of that community are made manifest.

> *I will value the ideals and special*
> *attributes of every library.*

The Bodleian Library

Here Greek and Roman find themselves
Alive along these crowded shelves;
And Shakespeare treads again his stage,
And Chaucer paints anew his age.
—John Greenleaf Whittier, *The Library*

I had the honor of speaking in September 2002 at an event celebrating the quatercentenary of the Bodleian Library of the University of Oxford. It was a daunting honor, rendered even more so by the fact that I was speaking in Sir Christopher Wren's magnificent Sheldonian Theatre in the heart of Oxford (and just across the road from the equally magnificent, if much younger, Blackwell's bookshop). The Bodleian is one of the great libraries of the world—a vast storehouse of the human record freighted with history and resonant with the memory of many generations of scholars. There was a library in Oxford before Sir Thomas Bodley, but it was not much of a library and had fallen into neglect by the time that scholar-statesman (1545–1613) turned his mind to his great library project. Bodley was a Protestant in an era when religious affiliation determined much about a person's life. He was born and lived abroad during a period of repression of Protestants in England and returned there when the tide changed and it was the Catholics' turn to be oppressed. He was a graduate of the University of Oxford (Magdalen and Merton) and later became an official of the university. Bodley left academia to pursue a successful career as a diplomat in many European countries and as a courtier attendant on Queen Elizabeth I. He

fell out of favor and left the court somewhat abruptly in 1596, then devoted much of the rest of his life to the project of creating the library that is named after him.

Bodley was determined to replace Oxford's decayed library of the time with a new library—"a most ample and commodious and necessarie buildinge." He spent money on the library, raised money for the library, gave books to the library, and persuaded many others (including Sir Walter Raleigh, Sir William Camden, and the Earl of Essex) to donate collections. The earl's donation was of a collection of books that he had seized from Bishop Mascarenhas of Faro, the grand inquisitor of Portugal, in what has been described as "a not untypical piece of Elizabethan book collecting." Bodley also pestered the first of his librarians—Thomas James—peppering him with letters on all aspects of library economy, from cataloguing to woodworms and from furniture polish to matrimony. (Bodley was against "his" librarian getting married, as he was afraid marriage would distract James from running the library.) After his death, Bodley left a fortune in endowments that laid the foundation for the great library of today and tomorrow. Robert Burton's memorial poem (translated from the Latin) tells us . . .

> *The well bound volumes shine in goodly rows;*
> *Each Muse her own appointed alcove knows,*
> *And is herself again, through Bodley's care,*
> *While what belonged to one, now all may share.*

I will appreciate the great libraries
of the world.

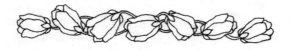

The Ventriloquist and the Boston Public Library

*Built by the people and dedicated
to the advancement of learning.*

—Inscription on the front
of the Boston Public
Library's McKim Building

The Boston Public Library was the first of the great city public libraries of America, the first publicly supported municipal library, the first public library to lend a book, the first to have a branch library, and the first to open a children's library. Its origins were stranger than most. Nicolas Marie Alexandre Vattemare (1796–1864) is not a familiar name now, but he was a figure of great cultural significance in his day. Vattemare was born in Paris and in his youth wanted to be a surgeon, an ambition that was stymied by his dismissal from the Saint Louis teaching hospital in Paris for misbehavior. That misbehavior consisted of many manifestations of his true gifts. He was an impersonator and ventriloquist of extraordinary talent. It was said of him that he could put on a play with ten characters and only one actor (Monsieur Alexandre, as he styled himself). He was a triumph all over Europe, attracting praise from royalty, including Queen Victoria and the Russian czar, and from public intellectuals, including Goethe, Pushkin, and Sir Walter Scott.

Alexandre Vattemare was a cultured man as well as a sensational performer, however, and he made a point of visiting all the art galleries and libraries that he could while touring. It was in the latter that he formed the idea that made him such a significant figure in the history of libraries. Vattemare had a

43

vision of a system for the international exchange of publications between libraries (and of art objects, coins, and medals between galleries and museums). This system became the dominant theme of the last thirty years of his life and he invested in it the considerable fortune he had made from performing. Though the French government failed to fund and support his scheme, Vattemare had far greater success in other countries, particularly in the United States, in which he was praised by no less a figure than John Silva Meehan, librarian of Congress. In particular, he impressed the cultural and social elite of Boston when he visited that city in the late 1830s and in the 1840s. Josiah Phillips Quincy, the grandson, son, and father of mayors of Boston, praised him as a benefactor of humanity, and Vattemare was a leading figure in the early discussions concerning the establishment of the public library there. The U.S. Congress passed a law on the international exchange of publications at Vattemare's urging in 1848. Though his efforts in international exchange were not entirely successful toward the end of his life, his legacy lives on in the global networks of exchange we have today and in the great Boston Public Library.

*I will honor the memory
of all library pioneers.*

Three

People

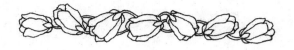

Colleagues in Schism

To a historian, libraries are food, shelter, and even muse. They are of two kinds: the library of published material, books, pamphlets, periodicals; and the archive of unpublished papers and documents.
—Barbara Tuchman, *Practicing History*

Librarians and archivists have many big things in common. They are both dedicated to collecting, making available, and preserving the records of humankind. They are divided by the nature of the records they collect, however. In general, libraries acquire published documents (books, periodicals, maps, videos, sound recordings, etc.) while archives consist of unique unpublished documents (manuscripts, unpublished sound recordings, diaries, institutional records, "home movies," etc.). There are, of course, exceptions—many libraries have manuscript collections and many archives contain ancillary published documents.

In addition, there are many small things that divide librarians from archivists. Probably the most important of these small things is their approach to cataloguing. Not only do they catalogue at different levels—librarians generally catalogue individual items, while archivists generally catalogue collections and files—but their whole approach to cataloguing is different. Look at a really small thing—measurement. Librarians record the height of books, the height and width of maps, and the dimensions of other library materials. Archivists generally

measure the number of shelving feet taken up by the collections they catalogue. Another difference is that subject cataloguing and classification are far more commonly found and are far more developed in libraries than in archives, in which the detailed subject approach is almost invariably absent. The two professions also adhere to different descriptive cataloguing codes—*AACR2* in libraries, variant standards (some homemade) in archives.

Thinking of these differences and about how important the similarities of mission of libraries and archives are, I came to the realization, to adopt an ecclesiastical metaphor, that we belong to the same church but are in schism. Library cataloguing is Catholic, with the Library of Congress as its Vatican and the rituals and pomp of *AACR2* its infallible text. Archival cataloguing is Protestant, with its inner-directed local variants, its many sects and practices, and its plain, practical, stripped-down records. We are, to pursue the metaphor, all engaged in the Lord's work—collecting, cataloguing, and preservation. Has not the time come for more ecumenism and harmonization in pursuit of that work?

I will value the shared mission
of libraries and archives.

The Life of the Mind

Life is just one damned thing after another.
—Frank Ward O'Malley

I recently interviewed someone for a position in the library. She told me that she could not imagine any place that would suit her better as a workplace—because she had always loved reading. I successfully repressed the hollow laugh that was engendered by that remark. It arose not least because I had said more or less the same thing when being interviewed perfunctorily for my first job as a junior assistant in a public library decades ago. I am sure she loves reading and the life of the mind; as sure as I am that I loved them then and love them today. The sad truth, of course, is that library work offers little to the reader and thinker apart from being around large collections of books (and even that solace is denied many library workers today) and that reading per se is rarely part of a library worker's job. There are a happy few—collection development librarians and children's librarians come to mind—for whom reading is part of the job description, but most of the rest of us are there to help other people find reading matter, information, etc. It is not long since that being well read was thought to be an essential qualification for a librarian, and Marian's glasses were an outward sign of the inward grace of being a reader. It is obvious today that being a serious reader is not a necessary qualification for high library office, and the remaining bookworms (itself an odd term with built-in disparagement) in the profession are generally confined to cataloguing departments, rare book rooms, and the like.

No, the model of a modern librarian is nearer to a technologist than a scholar. Nowhere is that more true than among library administrators. Their working lives are circumscribed by technology, budgets, personnel issues, contracts, building maintenance and repair, endless meetings, and the daily petty crises and disputes that constitute the warp and woof of management. In between reading memoranda and reports, writing memoranda and reports, attending or holding meetings about memoranda and reports, and writing reports of, and memoranda arising from, such meetings, the library administrator has little leisure to indulge in improving reading or to devote to the life of the mind. Perhaps the scholar-librarian was always a myth, but it seems that few, if any, examples of the type live and work among us today.

I will try to maintain the life of the mind
despite the mundane realities of life.

Micromanage This!

For forms of government let fools contest;
Whate'er is best administer'd is best.
—Alexander Pope, *Essay on Man*

Pity poor library administrators! At the center of their working lives there lies an insoluble dilemma making its presence felt every day. In all but the very smallest libraries, an administrator is perpetually torn between taking too detailed an interest in each of the daily activities of librarians and staff and being detached from those daily activities, relying on the maturity and the judgment of the people actually doing the work. In the former case, the administrator may be seen as caring and involved but is far more likely to be accused of micromanagement. In the latter case, an administrator may be seen as being a good delegator and someone with confidence in her staff but is much more likely to be seen as coldly indifferent to the individual realities of library life. So, which is it to be? Muffled complaints about interference and lack of confidence in the librarians and staff? Perhaps complaints about the administrator lurking in her office all the time and not caring about or understanding the tribulations of her overworked minions are preferable?

Library administration is not a career path that should be chosen by the thin-skinned or those with a deep need for unconditional love and respect. At the very least, a plentiful supply of children and dogs at home is required, since unconditional love and respect will be in short supply at work. Since, in these enlightened days, most administrators have lived another life as an actual toiler in the library vineyard, they should

at least be unsurprised by the criticism or even ready for its inevitable coming. Let us say that, in a hypothetical but realistic library, the automated system is proving to be completely inadequate, with an online catalogue that is inferior in many ways to the card catalogue that was trundled out more than a decade ago. Should the director decide that it should be replaced and with what, or should she appoint a committee to study the matter and come to conclusions? If the former, she runs the risk of being considered high-handed and dictatorial; if the latter, some might ask why she is being paid the big bucks and shuffling off decisions to the less well-paid. If, as is most likely, she asks a committee to make recommendations, the awful dilemma is merely postponed and indeed may be aggravated. The committee will, as all committees do, become invested in its conclusions and, if those conclusions are rejected in whole or part, become quite unhappy. Decisive or indecisive, dominating or malleable, the library administrator, in the words of the philosopher, cannot win for trying.

*I will try to understand the complexities
of library life and personalities.*

L. Stanley Jast

*The best inventions of America
are librarians on the one hand and
a martini in the other hand.*

—Louis Stanley Jast

Despite the best efforts of an ace reference librarian of my acquaintance, this quotation, which has turned up on the Internet a number of times (always without a source), has been elusive to pinpoint and authenticate. The faintly ribald tone (redolent of Groucho Marxism, Peter Arno, and the 1920s *New Yorker*) is completely at odds with what I know about the putative author. Louis Stanley Jast (1868–1944) was a public librarian in Britain (he was chief librarian of the Manchester Public Library) and a president of the [British] Library Association. He was a great innovator—among other things, he was the inventor of the bookmobile (he called it a "bibliobus"). A picture of him in a book of his essays published in 1938 shows a clerical-looking gentleman with piercing dark eyes, center-parted hair, and a luxuriant military handlebar moustache (he was the son of a Polish cavalry officer). He does not look like a British Robert Benchley or much of a martini drinker, come to that.

On looking into the book of essays, however, it is easy to see that this apparent sobersides was a widely read person of catholic interests, liberal opinions, and some wit. The book opens with a sonnet, first published in 1912, about that forgotten hero of the British public library movement—Edward Edwards. It then proceeds through many topics connected

with libraries and reading to a miscellany of essays on Shakespeare, the theater, the power of women in America, vegetarianism (he was against it), and endings in literature and life. One particularly interesting essay deals with his memories of reading as a child and the dangers of censoring what children read. The essay was published in the *Manchester Guardian* in 1928 and, in these days when we are grateful if children read anything at all, may seem quaintly old-fashioned, but the words ring true nonetheless.

> Whence my belief that a fairly normal boy or girl can read anything that is literature without ill effects; at all events that to forbid books is likely to have effects that are worse. There is a natural disinfecting quality in the unspoiled imagination of youth.

These were bold words three-quarters of a century ago; words that would be opposed today by those who would seek to infantilize children by protecting them from the horrors of reading the truth in literature. The fact that they were written for a national newspaper by an eminent public librarian in 1928 makes them even more remarkable.

So the mystery still remains, was Jast the eminent librarian also Jast the master of the quip? I am inclined to think so and like to think so—we all have many facets to our characters and underappreciated strings to our bows.

I will cherish the individuality and talents
of all my colleagues.

The Library "Character"

All things counter, original, spare, strange.
—Gerard Manley Hopkins, *Pied Beauty*

The thing that has amazed me most since my first library job has been the range of people encountered in any aspect of library service. I am not writing here of the "characters" that one meets among one's colleagues, but of the patrons, customers, users, or whatever the preferred term is for those who use our libraries. The eccentrics stay in the mind, of course. The second public library in which I worked (in the early 1960s) had a daily visitor called O. Pragnell (his library card merely bore the initial) whose pleasure it was to spend hours going through the drawers of the card catalogue looking for errors of filing, spelling, etc. His delight was to beckon someone from the desk and point out a misplaced card or one containing a mistake. (In the unlikely event there are any young persons reading this book, I must add that in those distant days many catalogue cards were typed by fallible typists. What is a "catalogue card"? I hear you ask, but have not space to answer *that* question.) That was forty years and more ago, so I imagine O. Pragnell is seeking errors in a Higher Catalogue these days. A few years before that a woman came into another public library to return a book and asked me, "Who wrote 'The quality of mercy is not strain'd'?" I did not know much then but I knew it was Shakespeare and told her so. "Not Ella Wheeler Wilcox?" "No, I am certain it is Shakespeare—*The Merchant of Venice.*" She then asked me for an eraser, opened the book to a heavily underlined passage attributing the quotation to

Shakespeare, and proceeded to rub out what she had written in the margin—"NO!!!!! Ella Wheeler Wilcox!!!!!!"—without apology or embarrassment.

I have not the space here to tell all the tales I have of the skewed, the strange, the eccentric, the kind (including an elderly woman who brought me homemade cookies twice a week because I "looked too thin," which, incredibly, I did in those distant days), the pedantic, the learned, and the just plain bewildered. There were a few horrid people, but surprisingly few out of the many thousands in many libraries over many years. One of the great strengths of libraries is that they are open democratic institutions in which all are welcome and only the broadest general rules apply. Within those rules, all can live the life of the mind, be entertained, study, do research, and pursue whatever avenues each wishes. The mind is free and nowhere freer than when in the library.

I will appreciate the many facets
of library users.

What's in a Title?

I don't believe anyone should lie about
[his or her] career history. But it's OK
to play with titles. For instance, one client was
a librarian, earning $27,000.
I suggested he should reposition himself
as an information management specialist. He
now makes over $100,000
at a consulting firm.

—Career counselor Nancy Friedberg

So there you have it. It is not what you do but what you are called, as this quotation from *American Libraries'* ever-interesting "Thus said . . ." feature tells us. It is inexplicable to me that a virtually meaningless term such as "information management specialist" should carry any cachet, but it cannot be doubted that the ancient and honorable title of librarian is losing its appeal to many. The word "librarian," as is well known, derives ultimately from the Latin for "book," *liber,* and "of books," *librarius.* Therefore, to the obtuse and the extraordinarily literal-minded, a librarian is, ipso facto, a person who deals only with books. To any sensible person, the word carries no such connotation, and those who call themselves "cybrarians," "knowledge engineers," and the like are justifiable objects of derision. After all, to a literal-minded person, a "computer" is a machine that does sums and a "computer scientist" is a sort of mechanical arithmetician. I have not yet met any computer scientist who is bothered by this possible confusion. Why then would any librarian feel bothered by being

called a librarian? I flat out do not believe that a person almost quadrupled his salary by changing his job title, but I stand in awe of his resourcefulness (and his employer's foolishness) if he really did pull off such a caper.

Even those who accept the title of librarian seem fond of renaming jobs and activities within their libraries (or "resource centers," "information centers," or whatever). I constantly see job descriptions, of academic interest only at my time of life, for positions with mysterious titles. What are "access services," "information delivery services," and "interpretive services"? The latter brings white-faced mimes (perhaps on unicycles) to mind. Now *there* is a new approach to brightening up the library image! The daftest example of this movement is the use of the term "knowledge access management" for a cataloguing department with bells on. The only library I know that uses this nomenclature refers to such things as "rush cataloguing" on its website. That is a shame, since "rush knowledge access," with its overtones of speed-reading, would be much more fun. Behind all the silliness, there is an important point. Our users are familiar with terms like "reference," "circulation," "cataloguing," "interlibrary loan," etc. Why sacrifice their convenience in pursuit of trendiness? I suspect that most users, confronted with a sign with arrows pointing in different directions to "Access Services," "Interpretive Services," and "Knowledge Access Services," would not have the faintest idea where to go for what they want.

I will use simple, easily understood
terms in all my work.

Librarians in History

There is a history in all men's lives.
—William Shakespeare,
Henry IV, Part 2

Most librarians are interested in historical figures who were themselves librarians. The term "librarian" is not always appropriate to modern circumstances, of course, and the likes of Casanova (librarian for thirteen years at the castle of Count Waldstein of Bohemia) and Mao Zedong (who worked in the stacks of Peking University as an "assistant librarian") would not qualify for a post that required "an MLS (or equivalent)," since the latter includes neither majoring in philandering nor leading a Long March. Mind you, Melvil Dewey (born Melville Dewey and a.k.a. Melvil Dui) would not qualify for such a position either, because he was too busy founding library education to actually acquire a library degree himself.

Other famous library workers have included the composer Hector Berlioz, the poets Henry Wadsworth Longfellow and Philip Larkin (who actually had a library degree), the fiction writers Jorge Luis Borges (Argentina's national librarian) and Alexander Solzhenitsyn (librarian in a labor camp), and six men who later became popes. The poet Archibald MacLeish was librarian of Congress and, by all accounts, better in that role than most of the academics and placemen who preceded and succeeded him. The fine poet Fleur Adcock was a government librarian in London, and Nadezhda Krupskaia (the wife of Vladimir Lenin) founded the Soviet library system. There are, of course, many women librarians who are notable within

the profession, but few who are widely known by those out-side librarianship.

According to their slim book *Blueprint for a Revolution*, Charles and Nancy Cook believe that the eighteenth-century librarian Francis Daymon should be better known than he is. Daymon, the librarian of the free library in Carpenter's Hall in Philadelphia, was employed by Benjamin Franklin, the library's founder, and served as an intermediary between Franklin and the elaborately named Chevalier Julien Alexandre Achard de Bonvouloir, a solitary spy in the American colonies in the employ of the king of France. At that time, within a year of the Declaration of Independence, such activity was treasonous, and Daymon and Franklin would have been in great danger if caught communing with an agent of a foreign power. Daymon not only arranged a meeting between the other two, but was also indispensable since one spoke no English and the other no French, whereas the French-born librarian was fluent in both languages. Everyone knows how crucial the French were to the success of the American Revolution, but few know how important the librarian Francis Daymon was in creating that alliance.

> *I will look for and cherish*
> *library heroes.*

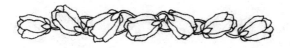

"The Amherst Tales"

*Curteys she was, discrete, and debonaire
And compaignable, and bar hir-self so faire.*

—Geoffrey Chaucer,
The Nun's Priests Tale

I have long nurtured the idea of writing a modern library version of Geoffrey Chaucer's *Canterbury Tales*. The idea does not appeal, however, to the deeply conservative people in ALA Editions, on whom I would have to call to publish my masterpiece. I would not go so far as to call them fuddy-duddies, but it is inexplicable to me why the publication of a long rhymed set of stories about librarians in medieval English does not strike them as commercially viable. Who could fail to thrill to "The Cataloguer's Tale," "The Tale of the Wife of LC," "The Children's Librarian's Tale," or the deliciously ribald "The Special Librarian's Tale"? My idea is, when I can find an enlightened, literary-minded publisher, that I would have a motley band of librarians set off on a journey, in a mobile library vehicle painted with flowers and peace signs, to Amherst to honor the great Melvil Dewey. On the way, they would discuss libraries and their lives, each taking a turn in telling her or his own story. I still think it would be an instant hit, vying with the Harry Potter books and even the second edition of the *Anglo-American Cataloguing Rules*.

I think that everyone has a story to tell and incidents in their lives that are of more than personal interest. What is missing, in many cases, is the ability to tell that story and recount those incidents so that people can hear or read them

with enjoyment. Additionally, even the most assiduous of biography readers can only read fifty biographies a year (one a week with two weeks off). We want to read and hear about people's lives but we must, perforce, be selective in doing so. For every amusing anecdotist, there are hundreds of pub bores, and for every well-written memoir, there are hundreds of turgid, unpublishable manuscripts. All human lives are interesting to at least one person, but few narratives of those lives enhance the reader's or listener's sense of life's tapestry. We live in a world in which the filtering function of publishers, which has worked so well in raising the quality of published documents, may be giving way to the "blogger" culture—an unending assault of unfiltered and ill-organized opinion and conjecture. If everyone's story is told, no one's story will be heard.

*I will be selective in my reading
and listening.*

Vartan Gregorian

A man of restless and versatile intellect.
—T. H. Huxley

The history of academics running libraries is not glorious. At best, such administrations are characterized by good intentions; at worst, by a damaging underestimation of the difficulties of the task and of the skills needed to be an effective head librarian. There are shining exceptions, and few shine as brightly as Vartan Gregorian. His lengthy and impressive curriculum vitae includes a stint as head of the New York Public Library from 1981 to 1989, in which position he can fairly be said to have rescued that venerable and valuable institution from pauperism. His is a remarkable story.

Gregorian was born in Tabriz, Iran, in 1934, into an Armenian Christian family of few means. One salvation was the small dusty library in Tabriz. Another was his grandmother, who inculcated a love of reading and learning in the precociously studious boy. As he writes of his early days: "In the books I read, I lived with great adventurers and lovers. I died and laughed with them. These books created a world to which I always aspired." That love of reading and connection to learning runs through the entirety of his fabled career first as a student at the Armenian College in Beirut, Lebanon, and at Stanford University (PhD 1964); in academia, culminating as president of Brown University; and in the wider world of public policy, most notably as president of the Carnegie Corporation.

Gregorian is what used to be called a "public intellectual," a man or woman of wide-ranging interests who comments on

public policy and intellectual questions of the day. He wrote a book on modern Afghanistan in the late 1960s—long before most Americans had any interest in or knowledge of that faraway country. His latest book is about the Muslim world and is a rebuttal of the "clash of civilizations" idea that has become so popular. He has commented on libraries, art, culture, politics, and education in a variety of media and places. His writings and speeches all reveal a deep belief in education and learning, both of which he says are more necessary than ever in a world "in which there is too much information and too little knowledge" (the latter an uncommon insight in most of today's public figures). He has been quoted as saying that libraries "rescued him" and is dedicated to spreading his own passion for education, learning, reading, and libraries.

I will learn and revere learning.

A Good Gray Profession

Grow old along with me
The best is yet to be.

—Robert Browning,
Rabbi ben Ezra

In her excellent and comprehensive survey of the graying of the library profession in the online journal *Searcher,* Becky Lenzini points out that as a group, only Elvis fans have a higher average age than librarians (there is, surely, a considerable overlap between the two groups). While a large proportion of the King's admirers are in their 70s and their pompadours are gray indeed, we are collectively the oldest of any of the professions. Ominous statistics abound. Only 12 percent of librarians are under 34 years of age, 63 percent are over 45, and more than a quarter of us will reach 65 in or before 2009. I have no statistics but suspect that some groups of librarians are, on average, older than others. Library directors at least appear to be. Everyone knows that there are far fewer cataloguers than there used to be—the single biggest misstep in librarianship in the last quarter-century—and I would guess that those who remain are even older than the average librarian.

Even among the traditionally "female-dominated" professions—teaching, nursing, and librarianship—we are older and less successful in recruiting young women, though all three have suffered declines. Stanley Wilder has compared the number of younger women entering librarianship with those going into the traditionally "male-dominated" professions of medicine and the law, both of which have shown staggering

increases in the recruitment of women under 30. In the case of medicine, almost four times as many young women are becoming doctors when compared to the overall increase in the profession. One does not have to be a trained sociologist to surmise that elements of medicine and the law that attract young, ambitious women include the salaries and status of doctors and lawyers.

If we are to reverse the negative trends in the librarian profession of the past few decades, we must seek to increase recruitment using a variety of innovative and productive methods, but we must also pursue campaigns aimed not just at pay equity but also at higher salaries for all librarians. We are a service-oriented, altruistic profession, but altruism alone does not feed us, educate our children, put roofs over our heads, or provide a just reward for our labors. One of the greatest improvements in modern society is that educated women are no longer restricted to the "female" professions—forced by society and custom to become teachers, nurses, or librarians. This is an unqualified good, even though it has added to the difficulties we have in recruiting a new generation of librarians to replace the large number of older librarians (and Elvis fans) as we swivel our hips into the sunset.

I will strive to improve the salaries
and status of librarians.

Four

Values

The Absurdities of Censorship

*The newer generation looks toward the
future unafraid, is interested and curious,
desires to discover whether the new may not
have more of meaning, truth, and beauty.*

—George F. Bowerman,
Censorship and the Public Library

George Bowerman's important paper on library censorship was read to the Washington Literary Society in 1930. Now, nearly seventy-five years later, much of it has great relevance to censorship today. Then, as now, the young wanted to explore the new and the radical, whereas the old wanted to keep "life, conduct, and thought in the old channels." Then as now, the new and innovative were feared and disliked by many, and that fear and dislike led to attempts at suppression in many communities. Then as now, librarians, especially public and school librarians in small communities, were caught between the warring armies of the progressives and the censors. Then as now, there was abroad in the land a "crowd psychology, compelling a certain rigidity and uniformity of speech and conduct." Then, it was the post-World War I mentality that informed the crowd psychology; today, it is the post-September 2001 mentality. In each time, it led to "crusades against the various grades of redness in politics and economics, against modernism in religion, against evolution in science."

You will note that though the Red Menace may have given way to the Terror Menace, enlightened religious thought and evolution are still under attack. Then, as always, the aim

of the censors was the suppression of the thought, ideas, and expression of others; not the promotion of their own thought, ideas, and expression. This latter point is a central issue in the struggles between censors and anti-censorship forces. The former wish to stop you reading or viewing things they do not like; the latter do not wish to impose anything on anybody—they merely ask for the freedom to read and view or *not* to read and view. Most strikingly, then as now, censorship produced absurdities. Books by Theodore Dreiser, Ernest Hemingway, Upton Sinclair, and Bertrand Russell, freely available all over the United States, were banned in Boston. Customs officials allowed Théophile Gautier's novel *Mademoiselle de Maupin* in French or in an English translation into the country but banned a Spanish translation of the same book. Conversely, the books of Pietro Aretino were banned from importation in 1929 in Italian or in an English translation, but the Spanish translations were not!

> *I will be aware of the follies*
> *of censorship and its dangers.*

Culture, High and Low

Every time I hear the word "culture,"
I reach for my Revolver.

—George Melly*

On the afternoon of the shortest day of the year, I walked to the library with my dogs to empty the book drop. As all who work in academic library circulation departments, but few others, know, the busiest time for them is the start of the holidays at the end of the semester. Almost no one is on campus, but those you see are laden with all the books they have borrowed and must now return. I have read of magical new book return systems that sort and check in the books, all the while handling them with the care of an automatic egg sorter. Ours is several generations short of that. The books are pushed through what is, essentially, a covered hole in the wall and land in a species of tub helter-skelter and with great wear and tear on the volumes. Left unattended, the result would make a book lover weep. So at these times, someone has to go to the closed library once or twice a day and rescue the books.

One of the pleasures of living in the great Central Valley of California is the agricultural bounty and the fields in which it is produced. In our case, there is a university farm north of the campus and, luckily for me, between the library and my house. That afternoon, it was dry and cold by California standards, if by no other. I knew that the local NPR station was broadcasting a dramatization of *A Christmas Carol* and looked forward to the walk and listening to the old story on my little

* This witty rewriting of Hermann Goering's infamous statement was made shortly after the Beatles released their album *Revolver*.

71

radio. After three-quarters of the way, as I neared the campus, the familiar words were interrupted by snatches of what I took to be Spanish-language rap. Eventually, the monotonous thud of angry words emanating from the student radio station swamped Dickens entirely. This was no great loss to me, as I know the *Carol* by heart, but the change in pace was abrupt and displeasing. I kept fiddling with the tuner at the low end of the FM band where NPR stations crouch, but I could not recover the station. I did find, in addition to the rap, a pop "country" station, and a fundamentalist preacher ranting about sin. He was against it. I gave up the vain search and turned my radio off. In a strange inversion, radio is now far more of a cultural wasteland than television. There are lots of rap stations, lots of preachers, and lots of "country" stations playing the kind of big hat acts that would make Merle Haggard or Doc Watson cringe. There are music for dentist waiting rooms stations and idiotic talk stations. In short, there is anything (except high or even middlebrow culture) available from 98 percent of the radio stations.

As I put the books on trucks to be checked in, I mused on the nature of popular culture and how easy it is to dismiss what you do not like and to resent the fact that what you do not care for is freely available and what you do care for is not. As an aging person I am irritated. As a librarian I must accept that we must provide and preserve the documents of high, middle, and low culture. We may know that Mendelssohn is preferable to Meyerbeer and both to Garth Brooks, but our libraries must collect all three.

I will overcome my own likes and prejudices
and be neutral in my professional life.

The Limits of Intellectual Freedom?

To limit the press is to insult a nation.
To prohibit reading of certain books
is to declare the inhabitants
to be either fools or slaves.
—Claude Adrien Helvetius

Most of us are committed to the idea that adults should be free to read and view whatever they wish and the concomitant idea that government, at any level, has no business dictating what any adult should read or view. The bitter battles are usually fought at the edges of these beliefs. They focus on such questions as the degree to which governments may forbid documents (in all formats) on the grounds of obscenity, blasphemy, and sedition or when governments and individuals should limit the reading or viewing of books, films, websites, etc., by children and young adults. Blasphemy and sedition faded from the censors' radar screens decades ago, though sedition has enjoyed a comeback of sorts in the post-September 2001 America in which I write. In a country in which more than 40 percent of the population are self-declared fundamentalist Christians, it is hardly surprising to find that there are a large number of people and organizations that seek ardently to restrict the reading and viewing practices (especially in areas touching upon the sexual) of "kids." (If there were ever a topic that deserves nuance, this is it, but the term "kids" covers both toddlers and people who are old enough to drive cars and own guns.)

So the dreary fights over sex and children go on interminably, with transitory victories and defeats and no changed minds whatsoever. Once in a while, however, a new issue comes along to lend spice to the debate. One instance is the case of *The Federal Mafia: How the Government Illegally Imposes and Unlawfully Collects Income Taxes* by one Irwin Schiff (a man apparently as challenged by English grammar as he is by federal tax laws). The Justice Department filed a federal lawsuit against Schiff (the author and publisher) on the grounds that he is "inciting others to imminently violate the law" (written by another grammar-impaired individual) and that the book should be banned to prevent revenue losses by the government and additional stress on the IRS. One might almost think that Schiff is a powerful advocate with a case that will appeal to many, for him to have brought the weight of the federal government down on himself like this. It is a classic case of an author's First Amendment rights colliding with the government's interest in enforcing the law. This in a country in which we do not ban books that tell you how to make bombs and illegal drugs and how to convert legal firearms into assault weapons, or that advocate the overthrow of the government. The crucial point, it seems to me, is that there is a world of difference between committing a crime and writing about, or even advocating, a crime. The difference between thoughts and actions is central to all censorship debates, and even those who want to restrict the freedom to read rarely dare to attempt to restrict freedom of thought, much though they might like to do so.

I will tip the balance in favor
of the freedom to read and view.

Patriotic Acts?

A patriot is a fool in ev'ry age.
—Alexander Pope,
Imitations of Horace

In the immediate aftermath of the awful events of September 11, 2001, the Congress of the United States passed, and the president signed, a 340-page anti-terrorism measure catchily entitled the USA PATRIOT Act. (The capitalized letters stand for "Uniting and Strengthening America by Providing Appropriate Tools Required to Intercept and Obstruct Terrorism," an outstanding example of misplaced ingenuity.) The act has been criticized on general grounds—that it was rushed through and voted on before its contents and their implications were fully understood or even read by legislators—but it is the invasions of privacy of the users of libraries and bookshops permitted by the act that have drawn the most fire. Put simply, the act allows federal investigators much more leeway in prying into the research, reading, and Internet use of library and bookstore patrons. Under certain circumstances, librarians are not only compelled to hand over such information but are also forbidden to disclose the fact that such an investigation took place. The act makes it far easier for investigators to obtain search warrants and subpoenas and increases the federal government's surveillance powers. It is interesting to note that a recent report shows that almost all requests to wiretap telephones are granted. There is no reason to believe that obtaining search warrants and subpoenas under the USA PATRIOT Act will be any harder. There is a "Son of the USA

PATRIOT Act" in the works that would further expand the federal government's powers and that has aroused much alarm in civil liberties and other watchdog groups.

Many local authorities have passed resolutions against provisions of the USA PATRIOT Act, as has the American Library Association. The most effective shield against this law is, of course, the traditional and necessary elimination of information relating to individual library use from circulation systems, computer caches, and the rest. The nub of the matter is whether this or any government has any business controlling or knowing about what people read, view, and think. And further, whether any such reading, viewing, or thinking has a direct correlation with actions—illegal, immoral, or neither. I believe that there is no such connection and that any attempt to sanction people for what they read, view, or believe is doomed to failure. In the meantime, precious security resources are being diverted from evil actors to this attempt to police those who have done nothing but *may* be contemplating bad actions. Jimmy Carter may have been self-convicted for lusts in his heart, but woe betide the government seeking to prosecute sedition in the brain or even the most immoral thoughts and dreams. Totalitarians of all stripes have been at that game for centuries—a game they have always lost in the long run.

I will protect the privacy
of library users.

The Bibliosphere

*Culture, the acquainting ourselves
with the best that has been known and
said in the world, and thus with the
history of the human spirit.*

—Matthew Arnold,
Literature and Dreams

Matthew Arnold was writing of what is now known as "high culture"—the very best expressions of the human mind and imagination. In this egalitarian age, such concepts hold little sway. For some, to say that Beethoven is "better" than Bob Dylan or Rossini "better" than Andrew Lloyd Webber reeks of elitism and snobbery. To others, it is quite natural to say that three of those named are great artists and the fourth is not—to them, judgment and taste point in only one direction. Viewed widely, the word "culture" is not something that we dip into and out of, but is rather a mental and spiritual environment in which we live. The anthropologist Wade Davis calls that environment the ethnosphere—"The sum total of all ideas, beliefs, institutions, and myths brought into being by the human imagination since the dawn of consciousness." The analogy is, of course, with the biosphere—a way of seeing the environment and all living things as part of a unified whole that is threatened by the explosive development and depredations of modern humans. In Davis's view, the ethnosphere is as threatened as the biosphere and by many of the same forces. Languages are disappearing and myths are forgotten or mutated, just as species are disappearing and animal habitats

are threatened. Equally, as physical losses in the biosphere imperil us all, cultural losses in the ethnosphere impoverish our mental and spiritual environment.

When one thinks about that part of the ethnosphere that constitutes the human record, it is easy to see that most of it— I call it the "bibliosphere"—is more resistant to loss than the other elements. An idea unexpressed dies with its conceiver; an idea told but not written down either dies with the person to whom it is told or is distorted in many retellings; an idea written on a single copy may or may not survive; but an idea printed in many copies or recorded on a durable medium can survive indefinitely in the same form as when first expressed. I see the ethnosphere as having many elements, the most durable and fixed being that part of the human record that has been recorded in many authentic copies (the bibliosphere); the less durable and more mutable being that part of the human record that has been recorded in single copies or electronic form; and the least durable and ever-changing being the words, myths, stories, and rituals that swirl around in our consciousness and semi-consciousness—the echoes of the whispers of the ancients.

I will understand the central
importance of the human record.

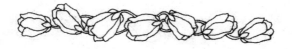

Rules of Conduct

Do all the good you can, by all the means
you can, in all the ways you can, in all the
places you can, to all the people you can,
as long as ever you can.

—John Wesley, *Rule of Conduct*

Could there ever be a more potent summary of what constitutes excellence in librarianship? We who work in libraries are animated by the idea of doing good by assembling, disseminating, and preserving the records of humankind and by providing assistance and instruction in their use. We are characterized by being restless and persistent in seeking new means of providing that good service to all, either through technology or innovation in other ways. We seek to use those means to create new ways of giving good library service. Libraries are everywhere, in communities large and small, and serve everyone regardless of their means, gender, ethnicity, or age. Finally, we never give up— individual careers wax and wane, but the library and the idea of the library go on forever.

The British prime minister Harold Wilson once famously announced that there was "more Methodism than Marxism" in the British Labour Party. The quotation above, from Wesley's *Rule of Conduct* (1784), shows the strong service ethic of the founder of Methodism—one that has animated the people their critics call "do-gooders" for more than two centuries. It is odd that the term "do-gooder" has come to be pejorative. Surely most of us would rather have good done to us than its opposite, and most would rather have a helping hand

than a slap in the face. Perhaps it is the strenuous nature of Wesley's injunctions that puts people off? (Wesley himself was a notably energetic person and prolific author for all of his long life.) Perhaps it is because they are a counsel of perfection—something that few if any people can hope to achieve. However daunting and exhausting the injunctions might be for the whole of life, they can scarcely be bettered as rules to guide all aspects of work in libraries. Following them, we will always be do-gooders by day, no matter how self-centered, imperfect, and unenergetic we might be by night.

I will seek to do good through
my work in libraries.

Looking Backward, Living Forward

It is quite true what Philosophy says:
that life must be understood backwards.
But that makes one forget the other saying:
that it must be lived—forwards.

—Søren Kierkegaard

Kierkegaard's short, sad, eccentric life was devoted to explorations of the meaning of life that usually ended in bleak conclusions. He was the founder of existentialism—a philosophy that prizes subjectivity and places the individual at the center of its vision of the world. There is something almost tragic in his understanding of the difficulty (or impossibility) of reconciling backward-looking understanding and forward-looking living. Later in the text from which this quotation is taken, he declares that he could never reach true understanding because the stress of living life forward would not allow him the perfect calm he needed in order to concentrate on looking backward. Less intellectual and tortured men and women reconcile the forward and backward paradox every day and wish constantly to illuminate their path forward with the light of their understanding of the past. Some of them (perhaps the majority) simply push forward, living the unexamined life and finding happiness where they can.

As with individual lives, our library lives have to deal with Kierkegaard's dilemma. In order to live the life of a modern librarian in a modern library and be effective, one has to have an understanding of what has gone before, of the history that has made our libraries what they are today, and the many

paths and bypaths we have traveled. To descend from the high philosophical plane, one practical reason for such understanding is to avoid the mistakes and blind alleys of the past. There are those, of course, who believe that library history is bunk and that contemporary technology will enable us to start over and jettison the past—to remake the library into something entirely different and original, a slate wiped clean. There are two problems with this approach. The first is that it flies in the face not only of library history but also of human history. Movements that have tried to remake societies utterly, leaving the past behind, have invariably failed. One has only to think of the French Revolution, which moved from a world made over to a traditional empire in a decade or so. The hideous tyrannies of the twentieth century—Soviet Communism, German Fascism, Chinese Maoism, the Khmer Rouge, etc.—all sought to obliterate history and all ended in failure. The second problem with the tabula rasa approach to libraries is that it manifestly does not mesh with the desires of library users. It is true that those users expect us to provide them with the latest technologies, but they also expect us to provide them with the books, journals, videos, and other carriers of knowledge and information they want, not to mention reference and interlibrary loan services, catalogues, library instruction, children's libraries, and library buildings that are vibrant places in their communities. How much more humanistic and sensible it is to strive to understand history, not erase it, and to try to live life forward at the same time.

I will seek to understand the past
and live in its light.

The Greater Good

The noblest motive is the public good.
—Sir Richard Steele, in *The Spectator*

The American Library Association's second task force on core values included the term "the public good" in its list of library values. Though it was not one of the eight values advanced in my book *Our Enduring Values,* I have come to believe that this idea is at the heart of any discussion of library values. Philosophers call this idea the public good, the public interest, the greater good, or the general will. The underlying theory is that it is moral and wise to seek a balance between the interests of the individual and those of the community in making public policy. Moreover, because healthy social institutions also benefit the individual, they satisfy both communal and individual interests. The greater good derives from utilitarianism (the greatest good of the greatest number), civic republicanism (republican virtue is expressed in the individual doing her or his best for the republic), and the general will theories of Jean-Jacques Rousseau. Each of these argues for an ideal state in which everyone works to better the community, yet all individuals remain as free as before.

Social conservatives in the United States are fond of talking about "culture wars"—a term that posits a divide between those who reject a paternalistic, militarist, repressive, and reactionary view of the world and those who accept that view. I believe there is a conflict that is wider and deeper than the "culture wars." There is a great difference in thinking and social policy between those who believe in the greater good

and those who believe in raw individualism. The former willingly pay taxes for institutions such as schools even if they have no children in the public schools, while the latter resent having to make such payments. The former see social investment in social institutions as good because society is improved when its citizens are healthy, educated, and literate. The latter do not unless those social institutions benefit them directly. The greater good is the overarching belief that underlies all our other values. It is a belief that is selfless, optimistic, idealistic, and progressive and that reconciles the rights of the individual with the greater good of society. It also provides the ultimate answer to the question "Why are libraries important?" The answer is, "Because libraries and librarians make vital contributions to all that we value about society—the greater good."

I will seek in all I do to further
the greater good.

Data Protection

The human animal needs a privacy seldom mentioned, freedom from intrusion. He needs a little privacy quite as much as he wants understanding or vitamins or exercise or praise.

—Phyllis McGinley,
The Province of the Heart

Privacy—the state of being shielded from the observation of others—is a relatively modern idea. It has its roots in the Enlightenment of the eighteenth century. Privacy is an idea that is central to modern librarianship, for both moral and practical reasons. The moral reason is that we have to respect the rights of individual library users to their own thoughts informed by reading and viewing whatever they wish, and we must assist their use of those rights in every way we can. There are two practical reasons. One of our central values—intellectual freedom—is challenged if individuals are inhibited in their access to texts and images because their use of them is subject to the observation of others. The second is that libraries, in a democracy, operate on the basis of trust and confidentiality. Without that trust, the library will never be able to render full service to individuals and communities. Citizens of repressive societies take it for granted that their library use is monitored and communicated to the authorities. Libraries in democracies must not only be, but must also be perceived to be, quite independent of government in their role as places in which minds are free.

The Canadian academic Colin Bennett has listed four aspects of privacy. First, free people should be free from police

searches, wiretaps, and similar invasions of their personal space. Second, free people should be free from intrusions by journalists and others seeking to publish private actions and thoughts. Third, free people have the right to make private decisions and not to have decisions made for them by others. Fourth, free people should control their personal information —their medical records, financial statements, library usage, educational records, etc.—and should be able to prevent that data from being used by governmental and corporate interests. This last is the aspect of privacy known as data protection and is the one that is most under threat from technological developments.

Many books and articles are being written about data protection because the computers upon which society now depends will, if not stopped from doing so, keep and store a record of every computer transaction. The big questions are: which steps should we take to stop this automatic record keeping, and how can we prevent positive uses of technology —computerized databases of medical records, for example— from being misused and exploited for repressive and commercial uses? In libraries, we must take some important yet simple actions to protect the privacy and confidentiality of our users. Computers will store every circulation transaction and every use of a library terminal for access to the Internet unless we write programs to wipe out the records of each completed transaction. Only those records that are essential to the running of the library should be kept. Those records should be generalized by the removal of the names of individuals when possible and those deleted when they cease to have an administrative use.

I will protect the privacy and confidentiality of each library user.

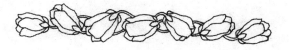

Civil Rights

The broad social responsibilities of the
American Library Association are defined in
terms of the contribution that librarianship
can make in ameliorating and solving
the critical problems of society.

—*ALA Policy Manual*

The American Library Association and librarians everywhere are and have been on the right side in the fight for civil rights of all kinds in the last hundred years or more. We stand for equality of treatment of all—members of ethnic minority groups, women, immigrants, children, the disabled, sexual minorities, and political dissidents. We stand for that equal treatment of the powerless and minorities because the logic of our values leads inexorably to that stance. How can we believe in democracy and intellectual freedom, in the right to read and think without interference, in equity of access, and in service to all without fear or favor, and not be among those who are counted when it comes to civil rights?

There are those who take a narrow view of librarianship and believe that we should only concern ourselves with MARC, turnkey systems, approval plans, management fads, virtual reference, and the like, and that we should stay away from anything that smacks of the "political." If librarians hewed to that belief, they would not have stood with those campaigning for equal rights for African-Americans in the 1950s and 1960s and beyond and would have lived without protest against the segregation that disfigured American society. If we

hewed to that belief, we would not have campaigned for equal rights for women and sexual minorities. Fairness is fairness and democracy is democracy and we should always strive, as we have for decades, to achieve fairness to all and an improved democracy. In that, librarians are idealists, because there is a measure of unfairness and a compromised democracy in every society on earth. It is not starry-eyed to accept those imperfections and keep on struggling to do away with them; it is not naive to think that society can be better and that we have a role in that betterment; and it is not unrealistic to expect that even small steps can lead to results and that librarians united for intellectual freedom and equity of access can be part of great societal change for the better.

Hubert H. Humphrey, a great campaigner for civil rights, was known as "the happy warrior." In his life and doings, as in those of Martin Luther King Jr., Cesar Chavez, Fannie Lou Hamer, and all the lesser-known heroes of the enduring struggle for equal rights for all, we can see that unbeatable combination of dedication to justice and unbounded optimism that has carried us this far and will carry us further. King said that the "appalling silence of the good people" was worse than the "evil deeds of the wicked people." We must play a part in social progress as librarians if we are to avoid that appalling silence.

I will dedicate myself
to equal rights for all.

Five

*Library
Services*

Many Tongues

Some hold translations not unlike to be
The wrong side of a Turkey tapestry.

—James Howell,
Familiar Letters

One of the universally received ideas about American society is that it is becoming ever more diverse and multicultural. Those who hold this view point to the number of languages spoken in this place or that and the way in which the United States assimilates people from all over the world, their languages, faiths, and cultural norms. In the long view, of course, this has always been the case. There were as many Yiddish-language periodicals in New York in the early years of the twentieth century as there are Spanish-language periodicals in the City of the Angels in the early years of the twenty-first century. Almost all of the Yiddish publications have gone, eroded by generational change and the suburbanization (which equals linguistic Anglicization) of the families who read them. Perhaps the Spanish publications of Los Angeles will suffer the same fate as the same thing happens to the Latinos and Latinas of that city and, crucially, their children.

Here is the paradox: the two trends are, first, increasing ethnic, religious, etc., heterodoxy; and, second, increasing linguistic conformity. Outside some niche markets and a handful of the largest cities, it is hard to find foreign-language movies or bookstores selling magazines and books in languages other than English. In this context, it is interesting to note that the current great interest in Arab societies particularly and Muslim societies in general has given rise to a great number of articles

decrying, among other things, the cultural isolation of those societies. Esther Allen has pointed out that the entire Arab world (population about 280 million) consumes only 330 translations each year, whereas the United States (population about 285 million) consumes . . . let us see, 330 translations each year (one-third of one percent of the titles published in the United States). If the cultural health of a society is measured by its exposure to thoughts and literature from other languages, the United States is in no better state than the Arab world. We can, of course, argue that since English is the most dominant language since Latin 2,000 years ago, our lack of input from, and knowledge of, peoples belonging to other language groups is no great loss. This is a culturally imperialistic notion that benefits no one. After all, are we better off knowing nothing of Arabic literature, culture, and art?

Libraries are pulled in (at least) two directions on this matter. We serve a mostly monolingual population, and the greatest happiness of the greatest number is served by the provision of English-language materials. On the other hand, most of us sense that the provision of materials from other linguistic areas (in the original and in translation) is of vital importance to the cultural health of our communities. Then there are the populations, served by many of us, that need foreign language materials because they cannot read English. In specific cases, this may be a need that will pass in a generation or two, but it is a need that must be met.

I will look beyond the English-speaking world for library materials.

Libraries Unplugged?

*It is the Age of Machinery, in every
outward and inward sense of that word.*
—Thomas Carlyle, writing in the 1830s

There was a vogue, some time ago, for the likes of Rod
Stewart and Eric Clapton to abandon electric guitars and produce an "unplugged" album with only acoustic accompaniment to their singing. Libraries have been plugged in for almost as long as rock 'n' rollers, and the idea of an unplugged
library seems as fanciful as that of a car that needs a crank
handle to get it going. There is, of course, a market for that
kind of automobile, fueled partly by nostalgia but also by an
appreciation of the styles of a bygone age. What would an unplugged library be like? Many users would hardly notice—
until they went to the circulation desk to check a book out and
were greeted by the kind of manual circulation system that we
all abandoned, with thankfulness, thirty or more years ago.
The reappearance of the card catalogue might please Nichol-
son Baker and his fans (Sid and Doris Bonkers), but would be
greeted by groans from our users and those with the wretched
task of filing cards in it. The return to printed indexes and abstracts would pose a challenge to all, but especially the young.
Used to finding something, anything, at the speed of light by
typing in random words and unused to the idea that a search
should yield consistent and accurate results, those young web
users would be hard hit. They would lack both the knowledge
and perseverance to comb through annual volumes and supplements using controlled vocabularies and, if they found

something, would be irritated by the inability to gain access to the article cited with a click. There is some evidence that many undergraduate students will reject anything they find doing a search in an online index if it does not give immediate access to the full article text online. It is much more likely that they would reject a whole system (paper indexes and abstracts) which lacked that facility. It is perfectly possible that they would be unable to interpret the content of the index entry sufficiently well to be able to locate the desired article even if they wished to.

Reference librarians in the unplugged library would be far less sedentary than they are today, since they would have to leave the desk to assist library patrons far more often than they do now. Cataloguers, too, would be seen out and about in the library—checking the card catalogue, authority files, and printed sources. Our systems personnel would either be twiddling their thumbs, sketching out futuristic systems, or tinkering with microform reader-printers. The library would have to find people with the kind of typing skills necessary for a time when the IBM Selectric typewriter was the ultimate in word-processing hardware. The unplugged library would be more of a nightmare than a dream, but thinking about it forces us to remember what we have lost as well as what we have gained.

I will value technology but
be aware of its drawbacks.

The Cataloguer

*Good order is the foundation
of all good things.*
—Edmund Burke, *Reflections
on the Revolution in France*

One of the great problems of modern library life is the shortage of cataloguers and the even greater shortage to come. The specialty of cataloguing used to occupy an honored place in our profession. No longer. It is under attack from all sides and our libraries are already much the worse for it. A large number of library administrators have grown up professionally in the era of OCLC and, lacking any real knowledge of cataloguing, have come to believe that OCLC will always provide and that there is such a thing as inexpensive cataloguing copy available at will. They, of course, misunderstand the whole enterprise that is OCLC—it depends equally on what all libraries *contribute* as well as what they derive from the nearest thing to a universal bibliography the world has ever seen. Those contributions can only come from original cataloguing contributed by professional cataloguers. The system simply does not work if libraries take and do not give. Then there is the failure of the successors to library schools to teach cataloguing or even to value cataloguing as one of the central parts of the professional canon. Much of the chatter about metadata (a silly concept that states, essentially, that we can achieve the benefits of cataloguing without cataloguing standards or cataloguers) emanates from the "information scientists" who infest LIS schools.

Caught between a library education system that does not value cataloguing and administrators who see cataloguing

departments as expendable cost centers, what is the cataloguer to do? We could start (I say "we" because I am not only a library administrator but also a lapsed cataloguer) by emphasizing not only the value of up-to-date coherent catalogues in an age of search engines, but also the centrality of cataloguing concepts and structures to library systems. Many of us have been through the agonies of implementing what we laughingly call a "turnkey" system (as if it were just a question of plugging the boxes in). The great struggle to specify every last element of such systems would invariably be lost were it not for the knowledge of cataloguers. Who else knows every nook and cranny of the MARC formats and how the umpty-ump field, %#$ subfield, differs between the monograph and serials MARCs? Who else can decide which fields are to be indexed and which are useful parameters for the numerous reports that the system promises to deliver at the click of a key? Libraries cannot exist without proper catalogues and proper cataloguers—it is as simple as that.

I will value
and support
the work
of cataloguers.

The Belligerent Librarian

I say to you, "you elegant fowls"
keep singing. Sing about books for children,
sing about reading, sing about poetry.
Hold out against too much benumbing
technology; revolt against mediocrity and the
cheapness of the quick appeal;
keep singing: charmingly, vociferously, softly,
and loudly, profoundly. And may
the singing never be done.

—Frances Clarke Sayers

It may surprise some to learn that both the title above and the quotation come from a children's librarian—albeit a very famous and much-honored one. Frances Clarke Sayers was born in Topeka, Kansas, in 1897. After training at the Carnegie Library School in Pittsburgh, she worked in the New York Public Library as an assistant in the children's room. From the beginning, she was renowned as a storyteller. She succeeded the famous Anne Carroll Moore as superintendent of work for children at the New York Public Library in 1941. She was a consultant to the Library of Congress and was instrumental in the creation of its Children's Book Section. She ended her career at UCLA, in which institution she was successively a lecturer in children's literature and a founding faculty member in the School of Library Service, which Lawrence Clark Powell established in 1960. She died in Ojai, California, in 1989.

Frances Sayers was a prolific writer and lecturer on children's librarianship, reading, and books. She also wrote a

number of books for children and edited children's anthologies. She gained a good deal of attention when, in 1965, she attacked the Walt Disney Company for watering down, distorting, and vulgarizing "books of high originality and depth such as *Pinocchio, The Wind in the Willows,* and *Peter Pan.*" (This must have been before Disney butchered *Winnie-the-Pooh.*) Her spirited attack was in the spirit of the happy belligerency she enjoined us all to practice. I suppose that to the terminally literal-minded, her use of the word "belligerent" to describe her professional ideals would smack of bellicosity and proneness to pick fights. The rest of us can readily see that she meant that we should stand up for ourselves, be robust in the promulgation and defense of our values, and proclaim the value of what we do. She spoke, in her 1949 address "The Belligerent Librarian," of "a profession that is informed, illumined, radiated by a fierce and beautiful love of books" and of librarians carrying on their profession with the "belligerency becoming to happy warriors." We are not as book-centered as we were more than half a century ago (for good and bad reasons), but surely we can recognize fervor in a good cause when we see it and seek to emulate the words and spirit of that happy belligerent—Frances Clarke Sayers.

> *I will be strong*
> *in standing up*
> *for my*
> *professional beliefs.*

Storehouse of the Human Record

For all knowledge and wonder
(which is the seed of knowledge)
is an impression of pleasure in itself.

—Francis Bacon,
Advancement of Knowledge

My wife is a keen fan of Edith Wharton's writing. She came across a reference to a Wharton book called *French Ways and Their Meaning*, published by D. Appleton and Company in New York in 1919, and requested it from our local branch of the Fresno County Library. That branch, named after Leo Politi (a famous illustrator and writer of children's books), is quite small and has a collection commensurate with a storefront library in a small strip mall. One might hope to find Wharton's *Ethan Frome* and possibly *The Age of Innocence* there, but certainly not a lesser work described by the author herself as "a desultory book, the result of intermittent observation, and often, no doubt, of rash assumption." Therefore, she requested the book through the interlibrary loan system after finding it in the catalogue of the San Joaquin Library System, which comprises a number of county and municipal libraries in the south of the great Central Valley of California. It turned out that the book, a slender volume with a green, gold, white, and red decorative hard cover, and in wonderful condition, was available from the central storehouse of the Fresno County Library itself. The label showed that the book had first been checked out in Tranquility (a small town in the foothills of the Sierra Nevada to the east of Fresno) and was due back on February 23, 1922. It was then checked out in 1926, 1938,

1940, 1941, and 1945. The record is then silent (in recent years, the system has produced a species of receipt showing the due date, thus saving the labor of stamping a due date label). It is possible that the book was checked out many times in the last few years, but it is scarcely probable.

So here we have two almost miraculous things. A serious reader pursuing a major American writer was able to obtain a minor work in very readable condition and in a timely manner. Also, a modest storefront library was able to satisfy a relatively recondite request. Let us thank the library gods that no vandal, bent on removing all books that have not circulated recently from the library collection, was let loose on Fresno County's collection. Let us also remember that our collections represent collectively an irreplaceable resource for humanity and that each book in those collections represents a triumph of the survival of the human spirit.

I will remember the value
of each part
of my library's collection.

Information Commons

Tomorrow to fresh woods, and pastures new.
—John Milton, *Lycidas*

The word "commons" refers to land held in common by a community, and in particular to pastureland on which everybody's animals may graze. It summons up an image of pastoral content, of a communitarian idyll in which each member of the community has the same rights as any other member. The word has been used metaphorically before to refer to shared property (including intellectual property) and is now part of the most fashionable of library phrases—the information commons. Rory Litwin has pointed out that this phrase is used to mean different things. One use refers to all the information in cyberspace that is available (at least theoretically) to all. In this sense, the "information commons" refers to our collective electronic patrimony. As such, it is reminiscent of the heady early days of the Internet, when the Web was seen as a species of cosmic, electronic Haight-Ashbury that would usher in an entirely new age of love and free information for all. This idealistic notion of the information commons will probably not prevail in the face of commercialism, state secrecy, etc., but it remains a powerful metaphor and provides us with a helpful way of looking at issues such as copyright and intellectual property. Another use of "information commons" is to describe places, services, and processes that promote the sharing of information unfettered by overly restrictive intellectual property laws. There is a legitimate area of dispute about which intellectual property laws are "overly restrictive," but here again we are dealing with important issues concerning digital information.

There is yet another more mundane use of the term "information commons." It refers to an area of a library, usually associated with a reference area, that is full of computers for public use. This meaning borrows from the moral force of the others but is, in this sense, no more than a trendy term for a dull reality. While those computers can be used for connection to the best of cyberspace and can lead to use of the library's staff resources, they more often are conducive to neither. A computer arcade used mostly for e-mailing, text messaging, game playing, online shopping, web surfing, and the other less-exalted aspects of the Internet is a far cry from any digital ideals. The taking of prime space in a library for batteries of computer terminals is a physical and symbolic expression of the primacy that many library administrators give to electronic information and data over the more organized and "difficult" manifestations of the human record. What we have is a reference library in which the most important reference materials—printed resources—have been relegated or banished and the reference librarian occupies a peripheral role. The sad thing about this is that it is completely unnecessary. I was discussing plans for a new library with a university administrator and he asked me, "Where's the technology?"—looking, one supposes, for a bank of computers in the center of the library. My answer was, "Everywhere." The plan is to have a wireless network and to allow all patrons to use laptops (borrowed or brought into the library) anywhere they wish and in conjunction with any other library materials. Technology is omnipresent as the tangible collections are omnipresent, to be used in privacy and as needed.

I will seek to use meaningful terms.

The Human Factor

People must help one another;
it is nature's law.

—Jean de La Fontaine,
The Ass and the Dog

The memoirs of the great and the good very often contain memories of libraries and librarians, usually from the authors' childhood or youthful years. I have done no scientific study of this phenomenon but my impression is that more than two-thirds of such references concern the impression left by individual librarians (the remainder being divided between reminiscences of library buildings and memories of the riches of library collections). Libraries can and do change lives, usually through the agency of individual librarians. Just think of your own school days—how often are your memories of subjects learned and of school buildings rather than of teachers and fellow students? At this distance I cannot remember a single thing I learned in the British equivalent of high school, and I would be quite lost had I the misfortune to be transported back over the miles and decades to that institution. However, I remember every teacher that I encountered (a few with fondness), just as I remember a reference librarian who helped me to find and interpret reference books about numismatics when I was a nine-year-old obsessed with old coins. It was, I believe, the first time in my life that any adult outside my family had taken me and my interests seriously. It was an act of service and an act of kindness to show a child how to find a nine-teenth-century German coin (bought from a tray in a junk shop for pennies) in the small print and cramped pages of a

huge tome among other huge tomes. The odd thing about that brief encounter is that the librarian probably forgot about it within the hour, whereas the small boy remembers it fifty-four years later.

This one-sidedness of memory imposes a burden on all librarians who work directly with library users, especially young library users. What if every transaction between a librarian and a young person were life-changing to the latter? What if all librarians were to be judged by how well and kindly each of us dealt with every question and every plea for help? We all have good days and bad days, and there are always times when it is easier to be dismissive or unhelpful than to treat every question with the regard that the questioner thinks it deserves. This burden, though, is also a great blessing because we are privileged to touch other people's lives and to help them in ways that we may never know simply by being kind, considerate, and professional.

I will treat every request for help
with seriousness and regard.

What Is a Librarian?

*I'm a librarian; I never see a book
from one year's end to another.*

—Philip Larkin, *Tracks*

The answer to the title question will vary depending of whom it is asked. Most librarians will tell you that a librarian is a person with a degree (in the United States and Canada, an advanced degree) from a properly authorized institution of higher education in something known variously as librarianship, library and information science, or even information studies. The magisterial *Webster's Third New International Dictionary* defines a librarian as "a specialist in the care and management of a library" and "one whose vocation is working with library books." (No hint of professional training or qualifications there.) To many, including many library users, a librarian is the last person they spoke to who appeared to be employed in the library. This last might be seen as a minor irritation if it were not for the fact that the popular definition of "librarian" leads to a popular attitude that ascribes only the most menial tasks to being a librarian and, hence, values the work of librarians not at all. We know we do good work, as do our more discerning and intensive users. However, if the rest of the world thinks the boogie-woogie Google boys are just as good as librarians when it comes to finding relevant recorded knowledge and information and that "librarians" are people who perform clerical, automatable tasks, it is small wonder that they do not want to pay librarians better salaries and that they nourish fantasies of virtual libraries.

For example, a group of robotics researchers in a Spanish university have been working on a "robot librarian" that has sensors, cameras, and grippers that can enable it to . . . do cataloguing? Answer reference questions? Conduct a story hour? Deliver library instruction classes? Manage an electronic database? None of the above, of course. The "robot librarian" is programmed to search for and fetch books from the library's shelves—not high on the list of librarians' professional activities. Then there is the case of the RFID (radio frequency identification) technology that uses chips implanted in books and sophisticated hardware to check books in and out. Some privacy rights campaigners are against the technology, while others argue that it will automate many monotonous and labor-intensive tasks. What it will not do is replace the work of any librarians. Despite that, many articles on RFID have said it will (to quote one) "liberate librarians from the monotonous and sometimes painful task of endlessly scanning books." By the latter they mean checking in and checking out, an activity in which few if any librarians engage. The same article asks, of self-checking made possible by RFIDs, if you want to "share your most intimate concerns with the librarian behind the counter." The idea of anonymous checkout is attractive, but very few mediated checkouts involve contact with a librarian. In short, when it comes to the public perception of the work of a librarian, they know not what we do. Perhaps we should be more active in promoting and explaining the complexity and professionalism of a librarian's work.

I will seek to expand the popular
understanding of our profession.

The Lapsed Cataloguer

Nice work if you can get it
And you can get it if you try.

—Ira Gershwin,
Damsel in Distress

My Uncle Tony—the Very Reverend Joseph Anthony Barrett, S.J., at the time of writing ninety-one years old and going very strong—told me, when I was a child, that there was no such thing as an ex-Catholic—you are either a Catholic or a lapsed Catholic. The idea that there were categories in life that you, once in them, could never escape entirely made a great impression on me. I think it is true of many other aspects of life apart from the theological and religious. It certainly is true of bibliophiles, of fans of the Chicago Cubs and the Rolling Stones, of politicians, and of poets. Perhaps it is true of librarians. I was amused to read an article recently in which an active member of the ALA Council, a person who works in the area of databases, was described as a "former librarian." I am fairly sure that she does not think of herself in those terms, and I doubt that any of us, no matter how far our work has strayed from libraries, would either.

More than a quarter of a century ago, when I was a useful and productive member of society, I earned my living as a cataloguer. Long before that, I had the great good fortune of going to a library school in which there were two inspired and inspiring teachers of cataloguing—Eric Stone and Alan Thomas. I had gone to library school in 1964 after working as a junior assistant (the lowest rung on the ladder of British librarianship) in two public libraries, with the fixed ambition

of becoming a reference librarian in a public library. Their teaching showed me that my real interest was in cataloguing and classification. In those days in Britain, all library students took a fixed first-year set of courses, one of which, called "bibliographic control" or some such, dealt with those subjects and launched the fascination that has endured to this day. In the second year, one could choose from a number of courses and I took all of those that related to "cat. and class." and left library school fired with the enthusiasm to be a cataloguer and to help in changing cataloguing standards. Largely through chance and dumb luck, I have had the opportunity to do both. My days as a cataloguer and my involvement with the formulation of cataloguing standards and codes were the most professionally satisfying periods of my life. I still think of myself as a cataloguer and nourish fantasies of post-retirement days spent cataloguing some rare and important collection. I believe it was the late Laurence J. Peter who formulated the rule that eventually everyone is promoted to the level immediately above her or his level of competence. As a lapsed cataloguer and current library administrator, I often have the uneasy feeling that I may be an illustration of Mr. Peter's rule.

*I will always remember
my library first love.*

The Death of the Reference Book

A shilling life will give you all the facts.
—W. H. Auden, *Who's Who*

Computers are very good at facts, data, and images (information), but no good at all at recorded knowledge. Standard reference books, the names of which are emblazoned on every reference librarian's heart, concern themselves with facts and data and, sometimes, images. Why then was it such a surprise to read a prophecy by my friend and colleague, Dave Tyckoson, that the days of the reference book are numbered, and that publishers of reference books would be well advised to seek another line of work? The flight from reference books by library users is quite explicable. As Tyckoson points out, people used to come to the library to seek facts, data, and images that were not available to them in their homes or places of work. Few came to the library to seek the weather forecast because that was freely available on the radio or television or in newspapers, but many did come to the library, specifically the reference library, to find data on the agricultural produce of Sumatra, pictures of the black-footed ferret, and short biographies of famous people. An industry grew up devoted to making profits by publishing almanacs, encyclopedias, dictionaries, directories, gazetteers, indexes, and abstracting services, all of which presented facts, data, and images in easily found, user-friendly printed form. This was a wonderful arrangement. Even the most modest library contained a ready-reference collection capable of answering factual requests on a wide variety of topics for its community. The great libraries with large reference collections literally contained a compaction of all the

information that humans had collected and preserved since the dawn of writing.

Those collections had two drawbacks—lack of currency and complexity. By definition, a reference book on all but closed subjects is out of date the day it is published—in the case of large reference books like encyclopedias, years out of date. The larger the reference collection, the more complex the search for information, the more sources to consult. Reference librarianship is not about, or even chiefly about, the answering of factual questions, though evaluations of reference always concentrate on that aspect, but reference librarians have become very skilled at helping users overcome the complexity of large collections of reference books.

Now the users have largely taken their inquiries elsewhere and the ranks of reference books, great and small, repose on shelves undisturbed for months or even years. The elsewhere is, of course, the Web. Despite the many shortcomings of search engines and the messy and inadequate results they usually produce, the populace has voted with its fingers and thumbs and seeks the facts, data, and images it needs from computers. *Caveat, Googler!*—the reference books may have lacked currency and may have been complex to use in aggregate, but they did have an attribute that much of the Web lacks—authenticity. The reader could be quite confident that facts, etc., once found, were accurate and from a reliable source, which cannot be said of much electronic information. This is beside the point, though, because we are set on exchanging authenticity for ease of access and currency and the reference book is fading into the sunset.

I will strive for accuracy and currency
in seeking information.

Six

Then & Now

Through the Years

Footfalls echo in the memory
Down the passage which we did not take.
—T. S. Eliot, *Burnt Norton*

A friend of mine suggested that my previous book of meditations—*Our Singular Strengths*—was a fragmentary memoir. Perhaps that is true and, in the postmodern sense, a set of short essays can be seen as the fractured mirror in which any author sees himself. Here is another shard of memory to add to the glittering pile. I started my work in libraries on October 1, 1957, when I walked up the stairs to the then Hampstead Public Library in Arkwright Road, London N.W.3, and began work as a junior assistant in the central lending library. I had no idea how lucky I was, of course. Let me tell you how long ago October 1, 1957, was: three days later the first man-made object to reach space—the Sputnik—stunned the world and changed all our perceptions—not to mention the impact it had on U.S.-Soviet rivalry. There were no computers, cell phones, videos, color televisions, fax machines, in-line skates, or modern photocopiers. World War II had ended twelve years earlier and hardly anyone had heard of Vietnam. Eisenhower had started his second term and Bill Clinton had recently turned eleven. It seems a strange world now, and the people there looked and dressed differently. Just imagine a time when men employed in libraries had to wear ties, dress shoes, and sports coats or suits to work and their female colleagues were forbidden to wear colored stockings or trousers. I well remember my first meeting with the man who was then one of the leading rebels in librarianship (later becoming an éminence

grise of the profession) and being greatly impressed by his denim shirt and scarlet knitted tie under a tweed jacket—an outfit verging on the scandalous.

Despite such restrictions, and here is where my great luck lay, it was a heady time for libraries, which were inhabited by people who were avid readers and deeply interested in culture of all kinds. A new novel by Norman Mailer or Jack Kerouac (we were all enthusiastic admirers of American culture then) vied with a new play by John Osborne or a new film by Fellini, Bergman, or Godard as *the* topic of conversation. This was intoxicating for a barely educated teenager out in the real world for the first time and it shaped, for good or ill, the rest of my life. I often wonder what would have happened to me without that magical time, but life is too short to waste time brooding on roads we did not take, and I never regret my library life.

I will cherish
my library memories.

1086 and All That

I've got a little list.

—W. S. Gilbert,
The Mikado

The Domesday Book is the record of the Great Inquest (survey) of all the lands and estates of England carried out at the behest of King William I (William the Conqueror) in 1086, twenty years after his conquest of England. The book contains a record of every estate and landholding, its value, ownership, area, tenants, livestock, etc. This exhaustive record was intended to last until the day of doom ("Domesday" is the Middle English spelling of "Doomsday") as the arbiter of all questions of land tenure and now provides us with our most detailed picture of a society in the Middle Ages.

The Domesday Book is held, as it has been for centuries, in the British government's Public Records Office. In 1986 the British Broadcasting Corporation (BBC) decided to create a computer-based, multimedia version of the Domesday Book, marking the 900th anniversary of the 1086 archive. The idea was to make a snapshot of England in the mid-1980s that would be as lasting as the original. To that end, the BBC embraced modern technology and stored all the data (text and images) it had gathered on two laser videodiscs with a controlling program that ran on an Acorn computer.

This was, you will recall, less than two decades ago. The problem is that both laser videodiscs and the Acorn computer are now obsolete, and all that data and rich multimedia information have been inaccessible for more than a decade. If you knew Middle English, could decipher such manuscripts, and

could be trusted with precious manuscripts, you could read the original Domesday Book more easily than you could view the 1980s version during the decade or more when it was technologically inaccessible. Scholars knew more about the landholdings of the late eleventh century in England than they did of the doings of many people still alive in the 1980s.

But all is not lost. The BBC has reported that a team of people from the universities of Leeds and Michigan has developed software that emulates the obsolete Acorn microcomputer system and the videodisc player and has made access to the 1980s archive possible again. This is gratifying, but one wonders how long it will be before another crack (and expensive) team of scholars and cybernauts will have to work on whatever system is being developed in the early twenty-first century to rescue twenty-year-old data? The Domesday Book's data is still here in the original manuscripts and on microform. The latter has many disadvantages, but having to be rescued after less than two decades is not one of them, and in any event, the original will be here for centuries after we are gone, as it has been throughout nearly a millennium.

I will cast a cold eye on technological
solutions to the preservation
of the human record
and understand their limitations.

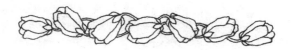

Libraries and the Internet

We look before and after
We pine for what is not.
—Percy Bysshe Shelley,
Ode to a Skylark

On the first day of January 1983, government and military users of ARPANET (a communications network that was the precursor of the Internet) switched to the recently developed Transmission Control Protocol/Internetworking Protocol (TCP/IP), and the Internet (short for Internetworking) was born. Seven months after that historic event, there were 562 Internet hosts; nineteen years later (in July 2002), there were 162,128,493 Internet hosts. Something far-reaching and unknowable in its ultimate effects had happened in a very short time.

Libraries are among the institutions said to be most challenged by this development. Certainly, we are challenged in budgetary terms. The public library has become the Internet provider to those who are poor and lack access at home, and it has had to fund that access. Academic libraries spend an ever-increasing portion of their budgets on access to electronic resources while striving to maintain their "traditional" and heavily used services. It is even said that many of those services might be replaced by the Internet and by entities other than libraries that provide (at a price) Internet services. This may be so, though it looks less and less likely as the years go by. A recent study by the Pew Research Center gives food for thought. It seems that the Internet has become "a mainstream

117

information tool" that many people expect to deliver what they want. The questions are, what is it that they want, and is their Internet use a threat to libraries? The four most popular topics and needs that people expect the Internet to deliver are news (69 percent of all Americans; 85 percent of regular Internet users); health information (67 percent; 81 percent); government information and services (65 percent; 82 percent); and shopping (63 percent; 79 percent). Libraries have never been considered a prime source of up-to-date news. They have provided general health information in medical dictionaries and the like, but the kind of health information (and misinformation) available on the Web is an enhancement to that service, not a threat—though reliance on it in preference to consulting medical professionals may become a national health hazard. I suspect that much of the use of the Web for government information and services has very little overlap with the use of government documents (printed and electronic) and, again, is a complementary service. Libraries have, at most, a marginal role in shopping and other commercial transactions. If these are the main uses of the Internet, how can they be seen as a threat to libraries? The Pew study is yet more evidence that library services and programs are complemented, not threatened, by the virtues and vices of the Internet.

I will analyze and understand the role of technology in modern life.

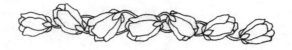

A Library Quarterly

*It has been suggested that not all librarians
are learned; but this is a calumny,
for learning of certain kinds being essential to
librarians, any librarian who does not possess
it, though he may accidentally draw a salary,
is not essentially a librarian at all.*

—Alfred W. Pollard

Those words were printed in 1901—hence the "he" embracing the "she," as wags of the time would put it. They appeared in an essay called "A Meditation on Directories" in volume 2 of the new series of *The Library: A Quarterly Review of Bibliography and Library Lore* published in 1901. Not much bibliography or library lore is to be found in modern library periodicals, and I do not suppose there is much of a market for either among today's librarians, but it is interesting to look back and get an idea of the interests of librarians more than a century ago. It might be imagined that a quarterly with that subtitle was a haunt of wizened old codgers muttering into their beards, but in fact it was edited by L. Y. W. MacAlister, then 45, a well-known medical librarian and founding father of the [British] Library Association. The other names on the masthead included Richard Garnett, then 65, the scholar and a leading figure in the British Museum Library; Carl Dziatzko, then 59, the great German librarian and author of the forbidding *Prussian Instructions* cataloguing code; and Melvil Dewey, then 49, the founding father of American librarianship.

119

There are 47 articles in the hefty bound volume (4 issues, 448 pages) of *The Library* lying in front of me. Sixteen are on various aspects of printing history and bibliography; 13 are on what was then known as "library economy"; 7 are biographical sketches (of librarians such as Dewey and literary figures such as William Morris); 2 are literary essays; 2 are articles on book collecting; and 7 are book reviews (mostly of catalogues and bibliographic works). Only one article is written by a woman—"American Notes" by Salome Cutler Fairchild. The reader can tell that the librarian to whom *The Library* appealed was a person keenly interested in day-to-day library matters (printed catalogue cards, public library statistics, the faculty library, etc.) but also capable of reading, with interest and understanding, about the sixteenth-century printer Luigi Cornaro, the *De missione legatorum Japonensium* printed in Macao in 1590, and forgeries in bookbinding. Not only that but, as the quotation by the bibliographer Pollard states, such learning was required of a true librarian.

Librarians today are also expected to be interested in "library economy," but their peripheral expertise and knowledge is very likely to be in areas of technology and management rather than traditionally learned pursuits. Who is to say that one state of affairs is better or worse than the other? Different times pose different challenges and call for different kinds of librarians. Though times have changed, perhaps the following (from the board of directors of the Brooklyn Public Library in 1901) in Salome Fairchild's "American Notes" may show that we have more in common than we might suppose:

> The board of directors . . . will not consider as a candidate
> for the position of Librarian anyone who has been trained
> for some other profession, and who has not had valuable

experience as a successful librarian. They will not accept some schoolteacher who seems to have missed his calling, or some minister who has missed a parish, or some bookworm who under the name of librarian has delved among library shelves, instead of making the library that he served a living fountain of knowledge and culture to the community about him.

La plus ça change?

**I will seek to understand the
continuity of librarianship.**

Another Library Quarterly

*Almost from its beginnings and to the
present, the library press as a genre has
been subject to severe criticism on the
grounds that, in Carnovsky's words, "much
of it is dull, repetitive, and worthless."*

—J. Perriam Danton,
in *Library Trends*, 1976

We have seen that the readers of *The Library* at the turn of the last century were as interested in bibliography and the history of printing as they were in what they then called library economy—the nuts and bolts of the practice of librarianship. I wanted to compare those interests with the reading matter offered by a library journal at the beginning of the twenty-first century. Estimable though *American Libraries* and *Library Journal* are (and they are greatly superior to *The Library Association Record*—the recently defunct successor to *The Library*), they do not offer anything of comparable weight and purpose. The nearest thing we have now is the *Library Quarterly.* The late and much-lamented University of Chicago Graduate Library School—in its day the intellectual and research powerhouse of American librarianship—started this journal more than seventy years ago. (Incidentally, Leon Carnovsky, quoted in the epigraph above, once edited *Library Quarterly.*) I took the four issues of the 2002 volume and analyzed the content with a view to discerning the differences in interest between serious librarians of today and of a century ago.

One feature of *Library Quarterly* that would appeal to the readers of 1901 is the different printer's mark featured on each yellow cover and the learned one-page note on its provenance found in every issue. This tip of the hat to bibliography is a grace note that seems out of place with most of the rest of the journal. Each issue contains three or four lengthy, serious articles and a large number of reviews. In the year under review, the *Library Quarterly* contained thirteen such articles (and another on the peer review process of *Library Quarterly* itself by the editor). Of these articles, six were on library topics (one on international librarianship); five were in the field of "information science"; one was on information policy; and one was an extended analytical study of a library thinker (Jesse Shera). You can see that today, as in 1901, the serious library reader is supposed to have interests beyond librarianship. Then those interests lay in bibliography, printing, and "library lore"; today they are in "information science" and information policy. It should be noted that the large number of book reviews and shorter notices (fifty-one in this volume of *Library Quarterly*) included many on bibliography and history—some on topics that would have interested the serious reader of 1901. An important difference between the essays of *The Library* of 1901 and those of the *Library Quarterly* of 2002 is that the former were quite accessible to the educated general reader, whereas the latter often need a command of an intensely specialized vocabulary. Consider the following:

> By thus accepting distance, and by undertaking an ongoing activity of textual interlocution, virtual communities enact the final goal of hermeneutics . . . As Ricoeur puts it,

"Distanciation is the dynamic counterpart of our need, our interest and our effort to overcome cultural estrangement . . . Reading is the *pharmakon*, the 'remedy' by which the meaning of text is 'rescued.'" (*Library Quarterly*, April 2002)

So there were challenges to the serious library reader in 1901 and there are different challenges in 2002. I suppose it is a matter of taste which set of challenges is to be preferred.

I will take a serious interest
in the literature of librarianship
and related fields.

Educating Librarians

Education is what survives when
what has been learnt is forgotten.

—B. F. Skinner,
Education in 1984

It is a commonplace to note, in the early years of the twenty-first century, that library educators are separated from practitioners by a gulf so wide that it seems that each side is speaking a different language. Indeed, the American Library Association has held three special conferences addressing this very issue in recent years. From the beginning of American library education in 1887, when Melvil Dewey established his School of Library Economy in Columbia University, to today—when the schools that used to call themselves "library schools" are busily dumping both the word "library" from their titles and education for librarians as their central focus—that separation has widened and narrowed and is widening again.

Let us look briefly at their history. Dewey moved his school to Albany in 1889, after a tiff with the trustees of Columbia over the professional education of women (they were against it, he was for it). By 1900 there were four library schools—at Albany, Drexel in Philadelphia, Pratt in New York, and at the University of Illinois in Urbana. The next decades were consumed with a largely fruitless discussion of standards and work on establishment of an accreditation process. What emerged was very like our current situation—few if any standards and a toothless accreditation system that judges these schools by criteria that *they themselves* establish. The glory days of library education began in 1926 with the establishment

of the Graduate Library School (GLS) at the University of Chicago and ended some twenty or so years ago with the steady decline into schools of "information," "information management," "information studies," and the like. During the golden age, teaching, research, and practice were far closer than they are now. Chicago's GLS, Illinois, Berkeley, Columbia, and others prepared generations of educated librarians, carried on much practical and applied research, held useful conferences, and issued valuable publications. The computerization of library work, the digitization of information, and the rise of a class of "information scientists" (mostly male) in the schools have changed the library education environment utterly. In many schools the faculty members who dominate are not librarians and have neither experience in, nor respect for, the practice of librarianship. Chicago's GLS and others proved that librarianship could be an academically respectable field of study in a research university while providing a steady flow of young librarians for work in libraries across the country. How are the mighty fallen! Columbia, Chicago, and Berkeley are no more and many of the remaining schools (with some honorable exceptions) are mostly cut adrift from libraries and the people who work in them. This rift shows itself in the fact that those courses essential to the education of librarians who wish to work in libraries (reference work, cataloguing, etc.) are now elective or shallowly introductory or both. The shades of Melvil Dewey, Katherine Sharp, and Louis Round Wilson must be weeping in the library Valhalla.

I will work to encourage
the education of librarians.

The Beginning of the Global Village

Ill news hath wings, and
with the wind doth go.

—Michael Drayton

In August 1883, the explosions that resulted from the volcanic eruption of Krakatoa in the Dutch East Indies (now Indonesia) reached their apocalyptic climax. Five cubic miles of rock were hurled into the air, ash fell as far as 3,000 miles away, giant waves (tsunamis) reached heights of 120 feet and devastated everything in their path, more than 36,000 people were killed (mostly by the tsunamis), the sound of the explosion was heard in Australia, and the meteorological effects were felt globally for three years after the explosion. Though not the largest volcanic eruption ever known (that was probably the even more devastating explosion in Tambora—also part of the Indonesian archipelago—in 1815), Krakatoa seized and has held the popular imagination to this day. I would cite the hugely successful 1969 movie *Krakatoa—East of Java* (Krakatoa is, in fact, west of Java, but that's show business for you) and numerous books and articles, some published in the twenty-first century.

The basis of this enduring fascination lies in an important stage in the history of communication technology. Krakatoa was the first major global event after the completion of the undersea telegraphic cable infrastructure. On May 10, 1857, there was an uprising in Meerut, India, against the cruelty of the British occupation of that country. It was the first violence in a dreadful series of events all over British-ruled India that became known as the "Indian Mutiny." Hundreds of Europeans

127

and Indians were murdered in an uprising that rocked the British Empire and led to many atrocities on both sides. The news of this event was published in the *Times* of London on June 27, 1857—a month and a half after it occurred. The news had to travel by ship. The first successful transatlantic telegraphic cable was laid in 1866—the reason why the death of Lincoln a year earlier was not reported in London until twelve days after it occurred. By contrast, the culminating explosion of Krakatoa occurred on August 26, 1883, and was reported in the *Boston Globe* on August 27, 1883. News of the explosion had reached the *Globe* in a matter of hours, and reporter John Soames became famous for a series of three articles in three days derived from the cabled news supplemented by assiduous reading in the Boston Public Library. It was the beginning of the global news infrastructure and the modern world in which we live. This world of 24-hour news, wars in living rooms, and lies circling the globe before truth has its boots on had its beginnings in the undersea telegraphic cable network that told of an explosion seen, heard, and experienced in about a twelfth of the world to the other eleven-twelfths.

I will understand the history
of human communication.

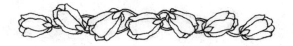

On the Burning of Books

Whenever they burn books they will also,
in the end, burn human beings.

—Heinrich Heine, *Almansor*

In the spring and summer of 1933 there were more than thirty organized book burnings in Germany. Most of the burners were students and members of the Brownshirts (the Nazis' private army). Alas, some of the burners were academics, academic administrators, and even librarians. The latter comprised both those cowed into submission and those with Nazi sympathies. The books burned were by a strange mélange of writers from Ernest Hemingway to Helen Keller, Albert Einstein to Karl Marx and Sigmund Freud, Margaret Sanger to Thomas Mann, and Rosa Luxemburg to Joseph Stalin. All were thought to be enemies of German culture (some solely because they were Jewish), and the burnings were aimed at the symbolic and actual purification of that culture. The Nazis were not the first (and will not be the last) to confuse the physical destruction of a book containing a work with the destruction of the work itself. The photographs and other images that survive of the Nazi book burnings are horrific testimony to the twisted delight in destruction that can infect humans in the grip of delusional ideas. The book burnings horrified the rest of the world and formed the basis of the first widespread understanding of the Nazis and the evil they represented. Much worse was to follow—the Nuremberg Laws, Kristallnacht, the Holocaust, the occupation of much of Europe, and the slaughter of millions in World War II. All were prefigured in the 1933 book burnings.

In the end, what did the burnings accomplish? As Helen Keller wrote at the time: "You can burn my books and the books of the best minds in Europe, but the ideas in them have seeped through a million channels and will continue to quicken other minds." Of all the books burned in 1933, not one has vanished from the earth and all are available to library users in America and Europe. It is hard to kill ideas and to "purify" cultures—certainly no amount of book burning will accomplish either. Lest we feel too comfortable, let us contemplate the idea of bigots burning manuscripts in the Middle Ages and depriving us of those ideas forever. Closer to home, let us think of the ease with which governments today can close down websites and databases they control. The Nazi book burnings were not uniquely horrific events, but only the worst in a long line of book burnings. On December 30, 2001, someone called the Reverend Jack Brock organized a "holy bonfire" in Alamogordo, New Mexico, and cast copies of J. K. Rowling's Harry Potter books into it to the whoops of a small number of his brainwashed followers. It was all in the name of purifying our culture, of course.

I will resist the burners and banners.

The Core of Our Profession

Profession . . . 4a: A calling requiring specialized knowledge and, often, long and intensive preparation including instruction in skills and methods as well as in the scientific, historical, or scholarly principles underlying such skills and methods, maintaining by force of organization or concerted opinion high standards of achievement and conduct, and committing its members to continued study and to a kind of work that has for its prime purpose the rendering of a public service.

—*Webster's Third New International Dictionary*

I apologize for the lengthy quotation from the great dictionary, but I think that this definition has so many points of interest in thinking about our profession—librarianship—that its length is merited. All librarians must possess specialized knowledge acquired through instruction in the skills and methods of librarianship and the principles and values on which those skills and methods are based. We certainly should maintain high levels of standards and conduct. Has there ever been a better definition of librarianship than "a kind of work that has for its prime purpose the rendering of a public service"? Much of the discussion of professional education that has occurred in recent years within and without the ALA has, more implicitly than overtly, centered on precisely the question of "what is a profession?" that is addressed in the *Webster's* definition. The fact that we have struggled to agree on a list of our core values and the core curriculum that should be required of library education is a negative indicator of our grasp of what it means to be a profession.

Nowhere is this seen more clearly than in the question of our professional body's lack of control over library education. This is not a failure but the result of unresolved philosophical differences. There was broad agreement until twenty or more years ago on what library schools (now library and information science, or LIS, schools) should teach. Skills and methods such as cataloguing, reference, collection development, the place of the library in society, and library administration were taught in all accredited library schools and were required of all library school students. What Guy Marco called "computer related-courses" began to encroach on these, as did teachers and courses sailing under the flag of information science. I recently read a list of the courses and research interests of the faculty of a major LIS school, and though I found remnants of the old core curriculum, they were greatly outnumbered by such topics as user modeling, information visualization, informatics, human-computer interaction, business taxonomies, strategic intelligence, social and organizational informatics, computational linguistics, electronic commerce, and computer programming for information management. Moreover, these newer courses and interests were centered overwhelmingly on the core faculty of that school. Two things have happened: the old consensus on the structure of education for librarianship has faded from view; and the concerns of the majority of the core faculty of most LIS schools are no longer the central concerns of librarianship. If we are again to conform to *Webster's* definition of a profession, we must reinstate the core concerns and ensure that they are taught in all ALA-accredited schools.

I will assert the core skills and
methods of our profession.

Bastille Day

France has neither winter nor summer nor morals—apart from that it is a fine country.

—Mark Twain, *Notebooks*

July 14 is Bastille Day—France's great revolutionary holiday, *le Quatorze Juillet*. As I write, I am remembering this day more than forty years ago when, as a nineteen-year-old with artistic aspirations, I was waiting in the Champs Elysée for a girl I had met in my local London public library who had told me that she would be in Paris in that place on that day and at that time. She never appeared, or maybe she did and was lost in the Bastille Day crowds. My friend Mac and I had left our jobs—his with a West End wine merchant and mine in a London public library—to travel to Paris with the goal of becoming starving, but ultimately acclaimed, writers. We nailed the starving part, but I can only think with a shudder of the slim sheaf of writing that I produced in the next few months. However, the sounds and smells of the Parisian streets and metro, the sight of the Seine and the booksellers on the broad banks on either side, and the working people of Paris in their *bleus,* are with me as vividly today as they were those decades ago.

It was my first trip "abroad," on the night train (the sign read "This way to the Continent") from Waterloo Station to Paris. We shared a carriage with three drip-dry suited American college students in Europe for their summer vacation. (Incredibly, one of them is now an eminence at the Library of Congress and still a friend.) One afternoon, I went in search of a public library in the *arrondissement* in which I was staying. It proved to

be hard to find, not least because none of the local people I asked knew of its existence or even seemed familiar with the concept of a public library. When located, it proved to be a dark, out-of-the-way place with a very small brass sign on its closed door. In retrospect, it looked like the private library of a nineteenth-century gentlemen's club—almost deserted with long, dark, slightly pitched tables and shelves so high that you needed a ladder to retrieve books from the two highest ones. There was an attendant, a man in a dark suit who showed not a flicker of interest in my being there, and no reaction to my leaving him alone to commune with his thoughts. That was all a long time ago, and many modern French public libraries are places of light, easy access, and attentive service (if in that uniquely French manner). However, the memory of that anti-public library lingers together with all the other memories of those months "abroad."

I will make my library
a welcoming place.

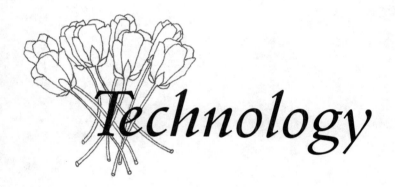

Seven

Technology

The Allure of Paper

One only has to look at any workplace to see how firmly paper is woven into the fabric of our lives.

—Abigail Sellen and Richard Harper,
The Myth of the Paperless Office

All writers know the awful moment when one stares at a blank sheet of paper or, these days, the blank oblong in the middle of the screen with its beckoning, blinking cursor. Many know the epiphany that comes when the words so painstakingly committed to paper or screen arrive printed on oblongs of paper bound into a book or magazine—and rendered authoritative, nay eternal, thereby. The authority and eternity may be only fleeting notions of the author, but it is the presence of her or his words printed on paper that works this minor miracle.

The ubiquity and popularity of paper arises, to a great extent, from practical concerns. Technologically savvy people print any text longer than a few paragraphs because they know that they do not like reading extensively from screens, they can make marks on the printed text that are not as conveniently made on the screen version, and reading long texts on paper is easier and better than reading on the screen. The latter is not based on custom alone but on real practical limitations. Humans instinctively favor the convenient and practical, and they seldom import inconvenient ideology into their private lives and the personal aspects of their working lives. Just as modernist architects seldom live in brutalist concrete edifices, even the most technophiliac informationists prefer books when it comes to lengthy reading, while prescribing

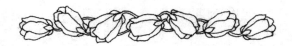

e-books to the rest of us. There are many books and articles telling us that flexible screens with high resolution that are "just as good as print on paper" are "just around the corner." The trouble is, that corner seems always just out of reach and has been so for more than a decade at least. That is why the "paperless office" has proven to be such a chimera. Anyone who looks at any workplace can see that there is just as much, if not more, paper than there was before mass computerization. Some futurists will say that it just goes to show how hidebound and reluctant to change we are and that future generations will live in paperless euphoria. This seems unlikely. For many centuries, humans have been making marks on clay, stones, reeds, animal skins, and paper with the idea of preserving those marks to be deciphered years, centuries, or millennia later. It seems unlikely that this quest for permanence will come to an end. The tremendous success of e-mail, if anything, reinforces this point. People are happy to use an evanescent medium for ephemeral messages but write letters when the occasion demands. To the writer, the word processor is a means to an end—the try at immortality through print on paper—an electronic pen that has replaced the typewriter, the mechanical pen.

*I will understand the value
and role of paper.*

The Dangerous Enticements
of Predictions

Di doman non c'è certezza.
(There's no knowing tomorrow.)
—Lorenzo de' Medici

One of the striking things about technological change in the late twentieth and early twenty-first centuries has been the thread of confident predictions of the future by so many. As usual, reality and predictions have not always run on parallel lines: many predictions have proven baseless, and many popular innovations have resulted from the unexpected and from unforeseen consequences. A few years ago, the gung-ho AOL faction trumpeted the far-reaching and glorious consequences of the age of the Internet and dominated the creation of the mega-conglomerate AOL Time Warner. Now their bubble has burst, that faction is gone, and the "traditional" media elements have taken over the company following the precipitous decline of its stock price. Thus, predictions that proved to be baseless have affected the lives and fortunes of hundreds of thousands of workers and shareholders.

The AOL Time Warner debacle, though spectacularly public and financially catastrophic, is just one example of a widespread phenomenon. Other examples can be found almost daily in the better newspapers and current affairs magazines. For instance, I noted three different stories in various issues of the *New York Times* in December 2002 and January 2003. The first dealt with the surprising, to the journalist, strength of the book-publishing industry. Item: U.S. publishers put out more than 110,000 titles in 2001, compared with fewer

than 40,000 in 1975. Item: trade (i.e., quality) paperbacks, university presses, and independent publishers are all doing well. This situation, familiar to anyone who follows the numbers, was not supposed to be. It was assumed that electronic books would be dominant by now. Instead, e-book publishers are going broke or clinging on to faddish niche markets.

The second article dealt with the decision by Columbia University to close down the company it created to provide courses and other material over the Internet. The failure of this ambitious enterprise (following the demise of similar projects at Cornell and NYU) is another manifestation of the perils of sinking large sums of money into projects borne along on bold predictions. In this case, Columbia (and thirteen high-powered partners) could not find a market for their digital content. We were told that the Internet was going to revolutionize higher education and make the "traditional" university obsolete. Visions of tens of thousands of fee-paying but distant students danced in administrators' heads. The truth is that technology is being incorporated into campus life, and Columbia University and the rest have far more applicants than they have places.

The third story was of a different stripe. It concerned the success of the digital archive created by the British Pathé Pictorial company. The company has made 35,000 hours of newsreels from 1896 to 1970 available free (at low resolution) or for a fee (for high-resolution reels and clips online or on DVD). Did anyone forecast the tremendous success of this and many other archiving projects in the "age of the Internet"? Did anyone forecast that making this unique historical record available free would stimulate, not depress Pathé's sales? Technology has many uses and strengths—most of them are obvious only after the fact.

*I will analyze predictions and act on them
only after much thought.*

The Quest for Authenticity

*1882: French futurist Albert Rolida
predicts sound broadcasting and argues
that there will be only one piano in Paris
by 1952 . . . in a radio studio.*

—*BBC History of Radio*

Monsieur Rolida is a perfect example of the perils of futurism. His predictions in this case turned out to be half right (sound broadcasting did happen) and almost humorously wrong. This is how his prophecy worked: since there would be radio broadcasting and radios would eventually be ubiquitous (both true), why would anyone go to the expense and trouble of going to a concert hall to listen to someone play the piano when the same experience could be had at home and at no expense?

M. Rolida, a man of some obscurity, was not alone in extrapolating a technological change to the point of absurdity. The same radios were going to be the main way in which higher education was delivered in the late 1930s. The talking pictures were going to be the death of live theater. Television was going to replace political oratory. Oops, that one did happen! That's the point, really. Sometimes predictions are dead wrong. Sometimes predictions are half right, and the other half is a real surprise. Sometimes predictions are mostly right, but with a skewed variation. Television destroyed political oratory and has almost destroyed political life, but the expected transference of the political arena to the box in the corner of the family room is not yet complete. Candidates still stump around the district, the state, or the country, traveling

thousands of miles, spending vast sums of money, and exhausting their physical and mental resources. Why do they do this when they could reach far more people via television without ever leaving their houses and television studios? I believe they do so for essentially the same reason that there are still plenty of pianos in Paris, plenty of books and magazines in plenty of libraries, plenty of concerts and concertgoers, and plenty of Broadway shows. That reason is the endless unslakeable human yearning for authenticity, for even the simulacrum of reality. We know that we can see more of the baseball game on television, hear that piano more clearly on a CD, and watch a musical on video at a time of our choosing. There is no substitute, however, for the reality of experiencing music played and plays acted by real humans in real space, any more than visiting a website is a substitute for reading a real book. It is easier to look at a picture of Yosemite than to visit Yosemite, just as it is easier to visit a virtual library than a real one, but no one can deny that the easier courses of action are sadly shrunken substitutes for reality.

I will prize the authentic
and the real.

The Changing Freshman

Knowledge is free at the library.
Just bring your own container.

—Anonymous

There have been many surveys of incoming college freshmen over the years. In the last decade, the surveys have shown a steady trend away from reading and studying books and other printed materials and toward spending time at a computer. It is said that the current generation of students (ignoring the fact that many current students are "returning," i.e., older) is comfortable with computers, even to the extent of being able to read lengthy texts from a screen. If this were true, it would be the most remarkable instance of rapid physiological change in human history. Reading from a screen is not difficult because it is unfamiliar to those used to reading print on paper; it is difficult because of certain irreducible optical and physiological facts concerning light, resolution, etc. One does not have to be a great cynic to assume that those students who gain information mostly from computers are not reading lengthy texts at all but are assembling whatever shards of information they can find to cut and paste them into papers. Another documented trend is students making far less use of printed periodicals and far more use of those journals, web sources, etc., that are available to them online. (Judging from the vast revenues from printers in my library, the first thing students do when they find such an article is to print it—presumably for ease of reading, highlighting, etc.)

These trends are certainly dictated by convenience and not by a disinterested search for truth. Many aspects of this process are troubling. The search engines (including the much-hyped Google) that students use to find relevant documents are notoriously fallible, presenting searchers with a random assortment of documents of greater and lesser relevance with no indication of how many other relevant documents have been missed. It is also well documented that today's students lack important critical thinking skills and (like the rest of the populace) tend to accept what they find on the Internet. This is much more dangerous than the acceptance of the printed word because the latter (provided it is at a level above the average New York tabloid) is far more likely to be authentic. Finally, the vast majority of the world's recorded knowledge (as opposed to data and information) is not available in electronic form and can only be found in the collective printed archive.

This is a time that calls for advanced and intensive library instruction. Every library should have such a program with at least the following components. First, include the teaching of all sources of recorded knowledge and information in all formats with their strengths and weaknesses. Second, teach a skeptical and nuanced approach to the use of the various means of searching and retrieving electronic documents. Third, incorporate a critical thinking element that teaches the assessment of authenticity and relevance of all retrieved documents.

I will teach the effective use
of all library resources.

Unitask Me . . . Please!

The shortest way to do many things
is to do only one thing at once.
—Samuel Smiles, *Self-Help*

I have always thought that the greatest modern invention was the clockwork radio—a device that enables people in third world countries to have access to radio broadcasts even when their electricity supply is sporadic or absent and in places where batteries are expensive and scarce commodities. This is a cheap, effective device—adapting the mechanism of the wind-up clock to power radios—that does one thing well and produces results without anything more than minimal human effort. There is a lot to be said for Walt Crawford's nominee for the greatest modern invention—the "off" switch—but I prefer the positive achievement of the British inventor of the clockwork radio, Trevor Bayliss. Companies now advertise cheap devices for sending and receiving e-mail (and nothing else) and cellular telephones that are designed to send and receive calls (and nothing else). These inventions and innovations amount to a quiet revolt going on in the world of technology. The revolt is, I believe, against the stress in life that is induced by the hideous demands of "multitasking" (a suitably hideous word). That ubiquitous combined blessing and curse—the cell phone—has always promoted multitasking. Its users can speak to someone else while preening and posturing and irritating all within earshot. Now the multiple tasks are increasing: new cell phones are not just phones but also computers, complete with tiny screens and minuscule keyboards, and

transmitters and receivers of photographs. I suppose the kind of people who announce "I'm on the train" on their phones now have no reason ever to get off the train, since they can hold their whole world in their hands. Now if only their phones could supply coffee!

Perhaps we too could consider joining the revolt against multitasking and cease to expect our library systems to do everything at once. Ever since the age of library automation began, the Holy Grail has been an all-singing, all-dancing integrated system. We have been echoing the fantasies of the Gatesites who essentially want human beings to live in and though computers, getting all our intellectual and recreational sustenance through a broadband connection. Just as real-life humans have shown a great resistance to living in or wearing computers, our library users show a remarkable ability to understand that, for example, each reference work is separate and concentrated on one purpose. Surely they could understand that a catalogue is a catalogue, an index an index, and a database a database, without expecting a magic machine to examine them all at once?

I will understand the purpose
of things and value them
for what they are.

The Never-Fading Image

They shall not grow old as
we who are left grow old.
—Laurence Binyon

I went to a funeral service the other day. It was more a celebration of the life of the community-minded woman who had died surrounded by her family in her eighty-third year. Her husband, children, grandchildren, and other family members elicited smiles as well as tears from the attendees in telling their tales of a long life well spent in family and social life. They spoke of her interests, her humor, her many benefactions of time and money in the service of others, and her indomitable, courageous spirit. The hour or so spent listening to these warm, heartfelt words was dominated by the picture they conjured up of a happy, good life, but it was also dominated by a large portrait of the deceased surrounded by masses of flowers just inside the chancel and the altar rail gates. The picture was of a young woman with blonde hair in a style that placed her in the late 1930s or early 1940s, wearing a simple sweater and a double string of pearls. She was, quite simply and by any standard, beautiful. Think of the young Grace Kelly. So we spent that hour or more listening to the achievements and joys of a long life while looking at a sixty-year-old picture of the surpassingly beautiful young woman who became the grandmother, mother, wife, and friend we were celebrating.

It has been said that no one is truly dead "as long as there is one person alive who remembers him or her." Perhaps that

147

can be extended to include "as long as there are vivid images of them or vivid descriptions of them in books." Viewed in this light, all writing, photography, filmmaking, recorded music, etc., are a dash for immortality. Is Marilyn Monroe dead when the world is awash in striking images of her? Is Martin Luther King dead as long as we can hear that mighty tide of a voice proclaiming the eternal truths of peace and reconciliation? Is Charles Dickens dead as long as we can open his novels and lose ourselves in the endless delights of the characters that he dreamed and infused with life? The fact is that we write words, make images, and record sounds to preserve a piece of life and art for as long as there are readers, viewers, and listeners who can reclaim that life and art and know what we know, see what we see, and hear what we hear. That is the awesome power of communication technology—to confirm immortality—and that is the awesome responsibility of librarians—to ensure the transmission of that immortality.

I will respect the power
of information technology.

What Is a Document?

I say that documents are, at heart, talking things.
They are bits of the material world—clay, stone,
animal skin, plant fiber, sand—that we've imbued
with the ability to speak.

—David M. Levy

Though the narrow definition of the word "document" is still in use—namely, an official record on paper—the word has acquired a far more expansive meaning in the context of modern communication. Even that wider definition was, until very recently, centered on tangible objects with markings (words, images, sounds, and symbols) intended to convey information and knowledge. Now the definition has to be widened even further. One of the fascinating things about communication technology is that each new technology tends to adopt the terms and jargon of previous technologies. Just think of the radio news announcer who begins her *bulletin* with "Here are today's *headlines.*" (A "bulletin"—derived from the same word as a papal bull—was originally an official announcement; and a "headline" was simply a printers' term for the larger-type heading that began a broadsheet or journal article.) In the same way, computerized communication has borrowed many terms from older communication media. One has only to think of "folders," "cutting and pasting," "web pages," "scrolling," "tabs" (derived from the tabulators on typewriters), and "bookmarks" to see the phenomenon at work.

It is small wonder that the concept of a document and the name itself were transferred into the world of the Internet and the Web. Tangible documents, on paper or any other physical

medium, have boundaries, beginnings, and endings. They have a shape and a physical presence. None of these traits are always applicable to computer documents. At this stage of the evolution of the medium, many computer documents are closely related to or even derived from their physical analogues. Sometimes this correspondence is 100 percent and a printing of a computer document is identical to the printed document. However, consider for a moment the computerized version of a daily newspaper. In the physical world, a newspaper may have many editions, each differing slightly from the others, but each of these editions has an unchangeable physical manifestation and will be the same tomorrow and, if preserved, in fifty years. The computerized version of that same newspaper is constantly changing, each change leaving no trace of the previous manifestation of that document. For convenience and out of habit, that computer version of the newspaper is assigned a day and date. In reality, it is an ever-changing work in progress and all that matters is the hour and minute when the last change was made. This is a document without boundaries, changing from minute to minute, unpreservable and uncataloguable. On top of all that, the computerized newspaper, because of the links and pop-ups it provides, exists in many dimensions. This is but one example of how things are changing. We have moved, like it or not, from mostly two-dimensional tangible documents with an immutable physical presence to changeable immaterial entities without beginnings or ends. They are documents because they record human thought and knowledge in words, images, sounds, and symbols, but we need entirely new applications of library techniques if they are to be preserved and made retrievable.

I will seek to understand the
implications of technological change.

150

Books of Photographs

*It takes a lot of imagination to be a good
photographer. You need less imagination
to be a painter because you can invent things.
But in photography everything
is so ordinary; it takes a lot of looking
before you learn to see the ordinary.*

—David Bailey

I can remember clearly the first time I saw a book of photographs. It was in a library, of course—my childhood home was bereft of coffee tables, let alone coffee table books. It was one of my semilegal incursions into the adult lending library across the hall from the children's library to which I should have been confined. I discovered that as long as you were quiet and cleanish and walked as if with a purpose, even an eight-year-old boy could enter the adult library without challenge. I found the folio books without knowing what a "folio" might be and was mightily struck by both the size of the books and their impressiveness when opened on the shiny table between the shelves. Over a number of visits, I worked my way from art books through flower books and books about pottery and jewelry and the like until the transfixing moment when I opened my first book of black-and-white photographs. I cannot remember the title or the name of the photographer, but I can see the scenes—of modern London—as if it were yesterday and not more than half a century ago. It was as if I had never seen lampposts, rain on streets, women in print dresses, buses, men with hats, children playing skipping games, or any of the all too familiar sights before. I have

151

thought that photographers—the kind that issue books—were magicians ever since that day. I was used to photographs—blurry "snaps" taken with box cameras and stiff studio portraits of people who clearly had to sit motionless for too long—but not to these huge glossy pictures that made the ordinary transcendent and a portrait the picture of a soul. Because that first encounter was with a book of black-and-white photographs, I have never had the same reaction to books of color photographs. They can be appealing, but to me they lack the visual impact and depth of the black-and-white image. The greatest photographer of the twentieth century—Henri Cartier-Bresson, who died in 2004 in his mid-nineties—photographed the famous and the unknown, great events and scenes of everyday life, and transformed all of them into works of art of great subtlety and impact. Yves Bonnefoy, who wrote the introduction to the book of the 1979 exhibition of Cartier-Bresson's work, puts the point well. "At first sight I conclude that here is something more than the reality which surrounds us. But at almost the same moment I realize that Cartier-Bresson's epiphany shines on a horizon that is common to us all."

I will value both images
and texts in books.

Filters

The medicine is worse than the disease.
—Livy, *Maxims*

The Internet is full of meretricious, vulgar stuff, but so are multiplex cinemas, most television channels, magazine racks, and all the other manifestations of mass media. Mostly, the latter are left alone, but as I write, the government is trying to impose the use of "filters" on public and other libraries, threatening to withdraw the federal money they receive from "e-rate" discounts and certain grants if they do not use filters on their Internet terminals. Filtering is an attempt to censor that relies on a manifestly disprovable idea. Filters consist of software written by for-profit companies that claims to block "objectionable" material from the scrutiny of the library user of the Web and the Internet while allowing access to the rest of the "unobjectionable" electronic documents. The technique used for this purpose is to search for "objectionable" words and phrases and to reject electronic documents that contain them. Despite claims by the filterers that they can write software that does this in a sophisticated manner, it clearly is not so. As anyone with a grounding in cataloguing and indexing theory knows, such precision is only possible when one is dealing with controlled vocabularies—that is, when a human being has examined a document and assigned terms from a thesaurus. Absent that, you are dealing with the myriad vagaries of the richest language the world has ever known—English. What is not generally understood is that filters operate on

exactly the same principles as search engines—free text searching—the first attempting to block, the second attempting to retrieve. Everybody knows that all search engines (the overpraised Google and the rest) retrieve masses of irrelevant materials and fail to retrieve a number of relevant materials, exactly as filters block things they should not and do not block things that they aspire to block. Given all this, filters not only do not work but also *cannot* work.

The companies that create and sell filtering systems are little more than confidence artists, selling their snake oil to soothe the anxieties of a gullible public and benefit from the scaremongering of right-wing politicians and religious figures. The latter almost invariably focus on "protecting kids," just as before the advent of the Internet they wanted to "protect kids" from comic books, *The Catcher in the Rye,* rock and roll, miniskirts, and whatever else was the fad for rebellious youth at the time. I believe a parent who encourages and rewards reading and discourages use of the Internet is doing far more for her child than any filter could. The ALA, in its principled objection to filtering, has been accused of a doctrinaire refusal to "protect kids," as if our reluctance to censor with a bogus technological response were morally equivalent to the motives of those who want to exercise their societal and religious beliefs to prevent the viewing and reading of things they deem objectionable. There is the fundamental and eternal difference—we believe that people should be able to read and view what they wish, they do not. Filtering is just the latest tattered banner under which the bigots and the censors march.

I will oppose censorship, no matter
which forms it takes.

Information Technology

*A world awash in information
is one in which information
has very little market value.*
—Paul Krugman

Nicholas Carr, writing in the *Harvard Business Review,* compared the explosive growth of information technology (IT) with that of other, earlier technological upheavals and reached some conclusions that run counter to the common wisdom about IT and its role in business. He points out that in 1965, information technology accounted for about 5 percent of America's business capital expenditures; by the early twenty-first century it was nearly 50 percent. Moreover, this rapid growth has led to a completely changed mental climate in the boardrooms of America. Chief information officers are as common as CEOs in the higher levels of business, and IT is seen as the saving grace without which any business will founder. Whole careers have been built on the idea that IT is the key to a competitive edge and is the central element of any business strategy.

Carr looks back to the way in which the world of commerce was successively changed by the steam engine, railroads, the telegraph and telephone, electricity, and the internal combustion engine. In each case the trajectory was the same. As each technology was being assimilated into the economy, windows of opportunity opened for aggressive people and companies, enabling them to build a real competitive advantage based on the new technology. However, those windows did not remain open for long. As the technology spread and

was made available to more people and companies, its competitive value declined. When everyone has a steam engine or electricity, those technologies become commodities. It is not that they were no longer important, it was just that they were equally important and valuable to everyone and, as such, virtually invisible. How many companies have a high-ranking "chief electricity officer" or a "chief transportation officer"? The absence of these positions does not mean that electricity and modern transportation are insignificant—in fact, they are vital to most companies—it just means that they are available to any company that can pay for them, and are part of the normal cost of doing business. Carr's idea is that the computer and information technology are on the same path; it's not that IT is unimportant; it just *is,* a fact of life that must be dealt with and paid for in every company. Crucially, a failure to recognize this is leading many companies to spend vast sums of money on IT to little purpose. For example, it is estimated that fully 70 percent of a typical Windows network is wasted. There are lessons in all this for libraries, almost all of which spend a higher and higher percentage of their annual budgets on IT and its attendant expenditures. We too are prone to be bedazzled by the allure of IT, to spend more than we should on IT, and to get too little in return.

> *I will understand and act*
> *on the true economics*
> *of information technology.*

Eight

Practicalities

Fund-Raising

Point d'argent, point de Suisse,
et ma porte était close.
(No money, no service,
and my door stayed shut.)

> —Jean Racine,
> *Les plaideurs*

Most librarians have little appetite for fund-raising, but most are experiencing ever-greater pressures to indulge in its dubious pleasures. Furthermore, most of us lack the skills to be successful fund-raisers. This might seem to be a small point. After all, have we not learned many skills over the past decades? Card catalogues are no more, and yet few of us had any problem adjusting to their online successors. We have, often overenthusiastically, embraced the Internet and the Web and left printed indexes, abstracting services, and other ancient tools in the dust from our chariot wheels. Anyone who has worked in libraries for twenty or more years has seen, and adapted to, more change than people should be asked to endure. The very term "information competence" was unheard of twenty years ago, but now many of us are teaching it to great effect. I believe that it was comparatively easy for us to adapt to all these changes because they arose out of the same culture and way of looking at the world that we already had. Fund-raising is different.

Libraries (with the exception of some special libraries in the private sector) are public-sector, "greater good" institutions. With libraries, as with schools, hospitals, places of worship,

law courts, and all the other appurtenances of a civilized society, the question is not whether they should exist, but what their nature and number should be. In the private sector—the area of life in which money rules—no institution is guaranteed existence; a product or service that does not sell is doomed to extinction. Even bookshops, with which libraries have much in common, only survive by stocking books that will sell, rather than books with other attributes. I believe the problem with fund-raising, even for the worthiest of causes—our libraries—lies in that clash of cultures. It is hard for someone whose whole life has been dedicated to service to all without fear or favor to learn the knack of cultivating people on the basis of how much money they have. It is hard for us to acquire the skills of salespeople not because those skills are beneath us, but because they belong to a different culture. We should always bear two things in mind, however. First, there is an aspect of fund-raising that can be most beneficial—the need to assess the strengths and weakness of your library in order to make a case for the funds you need. Second, this is a time in which public funds for public institutions are often insufficient to meet the needs of those institutions and, painful though it may be, fund-raising is likely to be a permanent part of most library lives.

I will do my best to ensure
my library is fully funded.

Maps

Geography is about maps
Biography is about chaps.

—E. C. Bentley

Of all carriers of recorded knowledge and information, surely the map is the most alluring. These stylized mixtures of graphics and text pack more information and latent knowledge into a small area than any other form of communication. These days, because of the sophistication of image technology, the two-dimensional wonders of the printed map gain other dimensions as the viewer zooms in and out or makes connections with other visual or textual data that are only a click or two away.

As a child, I learned and was fascinated by the conventions of maps—the blue rivers and lakes; the gradations of green to intensifying shades of brown and purple that are used for plains, hills, and mountains; the boundaries in red showing the shapes of counties, states, and countries; the difference in type size in the names of cities, towns, and villages—large for major cities and dwindling to near-unreadability for tiny hamlets; the way that capitals are indicated by stars and, appropriately, capital letters; and the mystic indicators of scale and distance. The wonderful thing about maps is that you can get something from a map even if you cannot read these various codes, and you can acquire knowledge of the codes gradually until you are capable of drawing all the knowledge and information that the map represents.

I have a huge map of California on the wall of my office. It taught me, when I first came to the Golden State, the immense

size and variety of its habitats and the areas of the state that are all but unknown to those who are familiar with the great sprawling coastal conglomerations of Southern California and the Bay Area, but who know nothing of the Inland Empire stretching 200 desert miles east of Los Angeles, the great Central Valley between the coastal range and the Sierra Nevada, and the immense green territory between the Bay Area and the Oregon border. All of these unknown Californias are there on my map, not only listed but also shown in their dimensions, placed in a way that appeals to the imagination as well as the intellect and sets the mind to dreaming of journeys remembered and yet to be taken. Those dreams and that knowledge are only possible because the viewer is able to read the graphic language as well as the text of this large, complex document. We carry the language of maps with us. Some are more fluent in it than others, but almost everyone can derive something from a map and learn lessons not easily forgotten.

I will continue to learn and appreciate the graphic language of maps.

Doing a Lot

Libraries that do a lot, do a lot.
—Hugh Craig Atkinson

Hugh Atkinson (1933–1986) was the most gifted academic librarian of his generation. The hallmark of his thinking and actions was the idea of cooperation between libraries of all kinds driven by technological innovation. He was an early and ardent supporter of OCLC when, in days long before its ideals were subsumed to corporatism, it was the most successful example of the application of computers to library work and the most successful cooperative venture in the history of librarianship. One of the things that Atkinson admired most about OCLC was the initial egalitarian principle that recognized the worth of all libraries and library collections. Large libraries have much to share with others, but the smallest libraries also have something to share. Since there are far more of the latter than of the former, the aggregate of the collections of small libraries, if harnessed by OCLC and others, is just as important as the collections of the largest libraries. Whisper it only, but OCLC, viewed clearly, is a triumph of the fundamental socialist principle—*from each according to his means, to each according to his needs.* This may seem an odd thing to write about a huge corporate monolith, but it is true nevertheless. Many of the faculty, librarians, and administrators in large research libraries are reluctant to engage in cooperative ventures with smaller libraries, especially smaller nonacademic libraries. That reluctance is based on the idea that their collections are of unique interest and hence their lending will be vastly greater than their borrowing.

Hugh Atkinson got national recognition for his pioneering work in the state of Illinois—work spearheaded by the gigantic University of Illinois Library, which he then headed. His great insight was that interlibrary resource sharing is not a question of small libraries taking advantage of large libraries, but of both classes of library benefiting equally—the small library from the resources of the large and the large library from the accumulation of one or two resources each from a vast number of small libraries. As it turned out, he was right. The University of Illinois Library lent very large numbers of books and other resources to other Illinois libraries, but was also by far the largest borrower—many years a net borrower. This experience led Atkinson to make the statement at the head of this essay—a statement that has the simplicity of truth. Libraries that lend a lot of materials and supply a lot of documents also borrow, acquire, catalogue, and preserve a lot of materials while providing access to a lot of electronic resources, answering a lot of reference questions, and providing a lot of instruction classes. Everything achieves balance if properly organized and run.

I will value
and recognize
the value
of every library.

The Curse of PowerPoint

*I do not object to people looking at their
watches when I am speaking—but I
strongly object when they start shaking
them to make sure they are still going.*

—Lord [Norman] Birkett

Has there ever been a more malign application of technology than the digitized slide show ("slidewear") called PowerPoint? One assumes it was developed for use in the commercial world to help salespersons jazz up their pitches, but it has metastasized into education and the professions, in which it has reached near-ubiquity. As recently as ten years ago, one could expect to go to programs at ALA and other library conferences and hear a more or less coherent paper, sometimes with the added entertainment of a few, initially upside-down, transparencies, but basically an attempt by the speaker to communicate a reasoned coherent argument with few distractions from the spoken word listened to attentively. There were, of course, poor speakers and poor papers (sometimes simultaneously), but shortcomings in presentation and content were soon exposed.

Then came PowerPoint—that last, best refuge for the incoherent, that series of dams on the river of logic and oratory, that exalter of form over substance. Instead of an organized speech with a beginning, a middle, and an end, we are presented, in a darkened room (thus eliminating the possibility of any rapport between the speaker and the audience), with a jerky sequence of slides containing a minimalist text (about forty words is typical), with lame and often irrelevant moving

165

visuals. Since it takes fewer than ten seconds to read those forty words—broken up into bullets—the mind is left to wander as the speaker repeats the words and then noodles on with her fragmented thoughts on the text. Click, flash, another slide, another vapid visual, forty more words, six more bullets, more noodling, another cycle, and on and on. So the dreary, disconnected torture goes on as the audience fidgets in the darkness, never finding what Virginia Woolf called the first duty of a speaker—"a nugget of pure truth to wrap up between the pages of your notebook." PowerPoint is killing the conference paper, reducing everything to simple-minded, fragmented, trivialized presentations that insult the audience when papers should be uplifting them. The Yale professor Edward Tufte has written the two best books in English on the visual presentation of information. He loathes PowerPoint and the "evil" it has wrought, criticizing it as a degrading influence on education and because it dominates rather than supplements the content of presentations. Small wonder he says, "Power corrupts, PowerPoint corrupts absolutely."

I will deliver
and appreciate coherent,
well-reasoned papers
and presentations.

A Virtual Alexandria?

*The library of Alexandria, founded around
300 BC or a few decades later, was the
first of its kind, and throughout ancient
history remained the greatest of its kind.*

—Lionel Casson, *Libraries
in the Ancient World*

The library at Alexandria in Egypt, founded by Ptolemy I almost 300 years before the Common Era, had a minimum of
100,000 "volumes," and one source estimates it had as many
as 700,000—defining a "volume" exactly is difficult for those
times of scrolls. We know it contained at least half a million
scrolls but not how many "works" or "volumes" were contained in those rolls. This great library was the center of learning and scholarship in the ancient world, attracting thinkers
and writers from all over the civilized world of that time. It
was the origin of many library practices that persist to this
day—including alphabetical organization and shelf listing. It
contained every work by the classical Greeks (many in numerous versions) and important works from other languages
translated into Greek. Some scholars say that this great library
was destroyed by fire in 48 BCE, others that it lingered on, far
from its former glory, until as late as 270 CE. In either event,
the great, comprehensive library of Alexandria stands as the
epitome of the fragility of recorded knowledge and of the idea
that all knowledge can be gathered in one place and then be
gone with the wind that carries the ashes of its carriers away.
The end of the library of Alexandria was an incalculable cultural catastrophe that resonates two millennia later.

Robert Dellavalle, a research dermatologist, has summoned the ghost of the library of Alexandria in a very modern context. He and some colleagues wrote a research report with numerous references, both to print and web sources. It was two years before the research report was published. By the time it appeared, a substantial number of the web references were to sites that had ceased to exist or had moved to other addresses. In short, many of the references he and his colleagues had painstakingly assembled to buttress their research were useless to the reader of their report. Intrigued and dismayed by this occurrence, Dellavalle and his colleagues studied the footnotes in scientific articles in three major journals—*Science, Nature,* and the *New England Journal of Medicine.* After three months, 3 percent of the web references in these articles were to inactive sites; after fifteen months, 10 percent; and after two years and three months, 13 percent. Other studies show even more erosion, more virtual fires destroying or making inaccessible still more recorded knowledge in digital form. Some commercial and academic entities are trying to create digital archives that are, in essence, snapshots of the state of the Web. However, these gargantuan archives, which we are always being assured represent several Libraries of Congress (in quantity if not in quality), cannot possibly keep up with the explosive growth of the Web or the equally explosive daily imploding of tens of thousands of sites. Still less has anyone solved the infinite problems of managing such archives. To Dellavalle, the parallel with the destruction of the library of Alexandria is inescapable—"things just a few years old are disappearing under our noses really quickly." We must find real solutions to this threat to the human record.

I will strive to preserve
the human record.

Animal, Vegetable, and Mineral

What is all knowledge too but recorded
experience; and a product of history;
of which, therefore, reasoning and belief,
no less than action and passion,
are essential materials?

—Thomas Carlyle, *On History*

The great Italian semiotician Umberto Eco wrote *The Name of the Rose,* a novel that will tell the reader more about libraries and librarianship and the value and power of recorded knowledge than twenty manuals of library economy and a thousand tracts on "information science." He spoke in November 2003 at the newly opened Bibliotheca Alexandrina in Egypt—that ambitious attempt to re-create the great library of Alexandria for the twenty-first century—about the human record and the ways in which humans remember and recall the knowledge of the ages.

In his speech, Eco divided our collective memory into three categories. The first is animal—the elaborate and unique apparatus of the human brain. The sorrow of this animal memory is that all the memories and knowledge accumulated in a life die with the individual, unless they are communicated and those communications are preserved. The second is vegetable—the memories of human beings recorded on papyrus (made from reeds) and paper (made from wood, bark, cotton, straw, and many other fibrous vegetable materials), each of which has proven to be capable of preserving knowledge over millennia. The third, and the most chronologically interesting,

is mineral. Everyone knows of the earliest records being incised on clay tablets or on stone (obelisks, stelae, monuments, etc.), but few reflect that we now store substantial chunks of the human record on silicon chips in computers and other mineral carriers (such as CDs) and that the apparatuses used to communicate those parts of the human record are entirely mineral. The paradox is that the early use of mineral materials is characterized by intense durability (so much so that the use of carving on stone to communicate, especially to commemorate, has never passed from the earth), whereas the use of silicon and other minerals in modern communication is characterized by extreme transience.

Another interesting feature of Eco's analysis is that the least permanent of the three forms of memory—the animal—is the one without which the other forms of memory are useless. A human brain is needed to tell human hands to drive a pen across paper, to incise stones, and to manipulate a computer keyboard. The texts, images, and sounds that constitute the human record with which libraries are concerned are the products of human brains and can be the extension of human lives years, decades, and centuries into the future *if* they are preserved for future generations.

> *I will seek to understand the*
> *nature of the human record.*

The Little Engine
That Sometimes Couldn't

What is the answer? . . .
In that case, what is the question?
—Gertrude Stein (her last words)

It is astonishing that the myth that every question can be answered by resorting to the Internet continues to persist, even though millions of people, wittingly or unwittingly, disprove it daily. In February 2004, the *New York Times* carried a feature called "When a Search Engine Isn't Enough, Call a Librarian." The piece opened with an anecdote about a librarian spending ten minutes or more online searching for the answer to a fairly simple informational question without success and then turning to a standard reference book and finding the answer quickly. There are two surprising things about the anecdote. The first is that the librarian did not go to the printed source first (we are told it was at hand in a "rotating bookshelf"—one hopes it was a rotating book*case,* as rotating shelves tend to spill their contents). The other is that it took so much time to answer a simple question online—it was "What is the name of the political party founded by Ross Perot?" My surprise is because that is exactly the kind of low-level inquiry for data or snippets of information that can usually be answered quickly by using Google or some such. In fact, if you enter *Perot + party* in Google, the answer appears several times on the first screen. There are, of course, 69,300 "hits," but 69,296 of them can be ignored safely. The basic point still stands, however: Google and the rest are wretched when it comes to answering more complex questions that are not susceptible to this simple word

171

matching that, despite all the hype and chatter, is the only thing that Google is good at. What if the strange but memorably named Ross Perot were called, say, Jim Smith and he had named his party "The Reform Movement"? Google returns about 380,000 "hits" to *jim + smith + movement* and about 900,000 to *jim + smith + party*. Even if there were a party buried in the 1,280,000+ haystack, how would anyone find it? What if the question were about the demographic makeup of Reform Party supporters in Illinois? (Remember that here we are still in the realm of facts and data.) What if it were about the psychological makeup of Ross Perot or the political and economic factors that gave rise to his candidacy for president?

The *New York Times* article points out that librarians are much better at searching using search engines than the average online surfer because, among other things, they understand the limitations of such searching and tend to be more skeptical (with good reason) of the results yielded by Google and the rest. However, the case for libraries does not and cannot rest solely on the idea that we exist to help people do better online searching and to teach them to use critical thinking when evaluating the results. The case for libraries is that we give access to recorded knowledge and information in all formats and assistance in the use of all formats. Online searching is good at answering informational questions, but the further you get from data and information and the nearer to recorded knowledge, the less useful that strategy becomes.

> *I will use all formats*
> *and strategies*
> *in meeting the needs*
> *of my library's users.*

Black Swans

Then she went her way homeward
with one star awake
As the swan in the evening
moves over the lake.

—Padraic Colum,
She Moved through the Fair

One of the most interesting papers on risk assessment in recent years is by the mathematician and financial analyst Nassim Nicholas Taleb. His theory is that the events that change the world and create history are utterly unpredictable. He calls those events "black swans" (on the theory that we expect swans to be white—unless we live in Australia, presumably). His fundamental point is that politicians, administrators, etc., make the mistake of trying to predict the future based on the extrapolation of current trends and the reading of current facts. No one has to look very far to find instances in which such predictions have proven to be way off in political, military, financial, and social matters. Library black swans come thick and fast, and our response to them is not noticeably superior to those in any other sphere. Who now remembers the glory days of DIALOG and BRS searching, when some librarians were hired primarily for their skill in mediated searching of those and other services? Did anyone in those days (less than two decades ago) see the coming of the Web and the transformation it would bring in the form of mass unmediated searching? Who saw the devastation of many school libraries that followed the tax revolt in many states in the 1970s and

173

1980s; or the explosion of communications media that has had such an impact on the collections, budgets, and services of public libraries? Universities and colleges are spending tens of millions of dollars in expensive wiring ("infrastructure") projects that have been planned for several years. What if the wireless revolution reaches its apogee and the libraries on those campuses are full of (a) people using a wide range of wireless devices to gain access to digital resources and (b) miles of wiring and connectivity, both unused? Whatever happened to the all-singing, all-dancing "scholar's workstation" in an age when the most valuable real estate in a campus library consists of a chair to sit on and a table upon which to rest books, notebooks, and a laptop connected to the wireless network?

Taleb's message is that we have to deal today with the repercussions of events that could not be forecast and will have to deal tomorrow with the results of events that cannot be foreseen. The message to librarians is that we should try to plan for the future not on the basis of forecasts that can only be accurate about small things, but on a determination to be flexible and adaptable in accommodating the unforeseen.

I will plan to be adaptable in dealing
with what cannot be planned.

No Child Left Unhurried

In reality, each reader reads only what is in himself.
—Marcel Proust, *Time Regained*

One of the unhappiest results of the national angst about public education is the growing obsession with tests. Testing and the comparison of scores between schools are seen as the solution to everything that ails K–12 education. Since free-form tests are too complicated and time-consuming to grade, almost all tests are in the form of multiple-choice questions amenable to quick summation (often computerized) resulting in a "score" that can be used to assess the progress of individual students and, in aggregation, of whole grades and entire schools. Maud's score goes from 68.98 to 72.46 on a 100-point scale and all is right with the world. The average score of children of Maud's age in the school declines from 71.31 to 69.77 and the teachers and the school as a whole are deemed to have failed. This mechanistic, antihuman view of human achievement completely fails to take the personality and talents of individual children into account and reduces the fragile web of teaching and learning to a set of meaningless numbers.

Take the case of "Accelerated Reading." This commercial product, designed to appeal to worried parents, school boards, and politicians with its illusion of science, is a computer-based reading program in which students read books that are said to match their own reading levels (and no others). They then take computer-generated multiple-choice questions on the facts in each book when they have finished reading it. The computer assigns points based on the length and reading level of the book and the number of "right" answers to the multiple-choice

quizzes. The totality of those points is intended to state, with scientific accuracy, how well the student is progressing in becoming a reader. Libraries are drawn into this system by being encouraged to shelve their books, irrespective of their content or whether they are fiction or nonfiction, in color-coded reading level sections. To the children being subjected to this inhuman process, each book becomes both an obstacle in a course intended to be negotiated at the greatest speed and a compendium of facts to be memorized, at least until after the computer has told them what their score is. "Good readers" (those who can read quickly and memorize the facts they read) like the system because it rewards them; "bad readers" hate it because it penalizes those who are slow to absorb facts, those who do not like reading, and those who like to take their time to appreciate the deeper messages of books that lie behind the facts presented therein.

This is such a horrible system that it is hard to decide which are its worst features. Making reading a chore on which you are graded is one of them. However, the ultimate sin against literacy and learning is the idea that a book is no more than a cumulation of facts and information. Is the joy of reading *Alice in Wonderland* to be boiled down to whether the hapless student reader can remember the names of the three sisters who lived on treacle in the bottom of the well in the Dormouse's story? Is a history of the Civil War to be deemed well read if the child can remember the dates of some battles? It would be far better if children were taught to appreciate the delights of the English language, the story of Alice and the stories that lie within it, and the big questions that gave rise to the Civil War than to be subjected to this computerized bean-counting that reduces joy and wonder to the banality of numbers.

I will try to instill the joy
of reading in all children.

Avert the Boots!

Spake full well, in language quaint and olden.
—Henry Wadsworth Longfellow, *Flowers*

In the early 1970s, I attended an IFLA conference in the French town of Grenoble. The hotel in which I stayed supplied each room with a posting informing the guests of the tariff, check-out times, etc., including instructions on what to do if there were an emergency. The most arresting instruction was *"In case of fire, avert the boots."* This is clearly the result of a mono-lingual French person who had a passing acquaintance with French-English homophones and near-homophones and was using a French-English dictionary. "Avert" means "to turn aside" in English but is similar to the French verb *avertir,* mean-ing "to warn" or "to inform." A century ago, "a boots" was a servant employed in a hotel to clean the guests' boots and shoes, and by extension, any lowly hotel servant. We were, therefore, being told to inform any hotel worker of a conflagration.

This long-ago story came to mind when I discovered a "service" provided by Google. The latter is, of course, the ubiquitous and marginally useful search engine that provides the user with a heap of answers (relevant and otherwise), in no particular order, to any question in the form of keywords. Google also offers a "translation" service for many retrieved items in languages other than English. For example, here is an extract from an article on cataloguing by my friend Mauro Guerrini found in Google in a version of English:

> The study would have regarded a wide beam of functions
> of the bibliographical records, is for the descriptive part, than

for the access points (name, tito it, subject, etc.), and would have produced a frame that could "constitute point of a clear, precise departure, very established and shared of that it is useful to the bibliographical record in order to supply the information and that that is thought necessary because the record answers to the requirements of customer."

The search for machine translation without human intervention has been going on for decades, yet this kind of thing is still the best they can do. That search is similar to the quest for a search engine that will deliver results that are as good as an adequate library catalogue—that is, search results that are relevant and complete and are presented in a useful order. Both of these quests are doomed to disappointment because they ignore the vital role that shaping human minds play in both translating and cataloguing. Without those human minds, good translations are as impossible as good cataloguing. We should accept that idea and embrace it instead of pursuing the fool's gold of mechanical cataloguing and automatic translation.

I will understand the practical
limitations of technology.

Nine

The Eightfold Path

The Fourth Noble Truth

Divine melodious truth.

—John Keats

Gautama Buddha (named Siddhartha at birth) lived in India for eighty years, from approximately 563 to 483 BCE. His teachings are based on the enlightenment (Buddhahood) that he achieved at the age of thirty-five. Those teachings are based on four "noble truths": life is sorrow; sorrow has a cause; sorrow can be transcended; and the way to the transcendence of sorrow lies in what the Buddha called the Eightfold Path. That path has three main parts: moral conduct (*sila*), concentration or meditation (*samadhi*), and wisdom (*prajna*). Each of these parts has components that together comprise the Eightfold Path. Those components are:

right view	right livelihood
right intention	right effort
right speech	right mindfulness
right action	right concentration

This concentrated version of the Buddhist discipline exists not only on the spiritual and religious level, but also as a guide to conduct that leads to a good and fulfilled life. I am particularly interested in the ethical aspects of the Buddhist Eightfold Path and am going to attempt to relate each of them to librarianship, especially the ethics and values of librarianship, in the rest of the essays in this chapter. To the Buddha, an individual life was brief and full of "sorrow," by which he meant the disappointment and despair inevitably caused by cravings for the transient things of the world. It may seem almost paradoxical

181

that the Buddha's Middle Way rejects not only self-indulgence but also extreme asceticism, but in fact both are two sides of the same coin—they are both centered on the self and are not concerned with the moral, well-conducted life. In the Middle Way, the person seeking enlightenment is in control of her or his own destiny, is self-reliant, and is in control of his or her own welfare. The lesson for librarians is that we should see beyond the day-to-day exigencies and the transitory pleasures of our library lives and seek to act in the correct way with an eye to the permanence of the library, the transcendence of the human record, and the search for enduring knowledge.

*I will seek balance and take
the long view in my library life.*

Right View and Right Understanding

See all, nor be afraid.

—Robert Browning,
Rabbi ben Ezra

Right view is one of the components of the Buddhist discipline of intuitive wisdom or insight (*prajna*) gained through concentration and meditation. These last are not ends in themselves but means to an end, which is to see things as they really are. Meditation is used widely as a religious discipline and in a nonreligious context as a means to relaxation and overcoming stress. In this case, it is a means to true knowledge by clearing the mind of the ephemeral and unimportant. One book on Buddhism recommends certain optimal physical surroundings as conducive to the concentration needed to see things as they are—a forest, the root of a tree, a hilltop, a mountain cave—but stresses that meditation and concentration are available to anyone who can clear her or his mind of the mental hindrances that impede us all—longing for worldly things, malice, laziness, distraction and anxiety, doubt.

If you wish to think clearly about library life as it is, it is important to rid the mind of those hindrances. For example, it is hard to think about plans for a new library service if you are constrained by a desire for self-advancement, by malice toward any of the people involved, a distaste for the effort that clear thinking involves, the distraction of other issues in the library, stress caused by job overload, or doubt as to whether the new services can be accomplished. Among the thousands of librarians I have known, one librarian was a Buddhist monk and another may have been a saint, but the vast majority of us

183

are neither monks nor saints. We lack the mental discipline of the former and the divine benevolence of the latter. Our working lives are full of what a Buddhist would call "sorrow" engendered by personal conflicts, stress, and doubts, not to mention ever-present budget woes. Not only are these distractions and hindrances ever present, but they also impede us from thinking about how to make things better. It may sound impractical, but I would urge all my colleagues to find time for concentration on the important issues that face them. You do not have to assume the lotus position and engage in deep meditation and the four levels of trance available to adepts to see things in the library as they really are. All that is necessary is the ability to do two things: put aside the personalities and other distractions of daily library life and focus on the reality of the issue at hand.

*I will concentrate
on the real issues
of my library life.*

Right-Directed Thought

A single word even may be a spark
of inextinguishable thought.

—Percy Bysshe Shelley,
A Defence of Poetry

Right-directed thought (sometimes called "right intention") is the second of the two components of the Buddhist discipline of intuitive wisdom or insight (*prajna*). The ultimate aim of the discipline is to reach a state of transcendent wisdom through meditation and concentration, not only by seeing things as they are but also through concentration on directing thoughts away from the unimportant and the transitory and to the eternal and the true. Right-directed thought is concerned not with the self and the ego or the surface of life but with the deep and important things of life. Buddhist writings frequently portray the undisciplined mind as being like a monkey that always jumps from one thing to another and never stays with one topic. The point of training the mind is to avoid that kind of scattered thinking.

It is not at all hard to see useful applications of right-directed thought in librarianship. Impermanence is to be found in examples such as technological innovation for its own sake, imperfect collection development policies that do not distinguish between ephemeral publications and those of permanent value, or overspending on a special project, and is always to be avoided. Moreover, such weaknesses are almost always the result of thought and planning being misdirected. Librarians should always direct their thoughts to the big issues and enduring themes of our profession—intellectual freedom, the

onward transmission of the human record, service to our communities, etc.—and not be concerned with transitory issues that cloud or obstruct our progress toward important goals. We plan and erect buildings to provide library service; we create collection development policies to buy materials that are of use and value; we purchase computers, software, and access to databases in order to give library users access to data and information that would not otherwise be available; and we have information competence and library instruction programs in order to empower our users and improve their lives. In each case it is the end that is important, not the means, and right-directed thought is always focused on those ends. To the extent that we are concerned with form rather than content and means rather than ends, it should always be to ensure that we are using the best and most efficient means to predetermined ends.

I will concentrate
on the important
and valuable aspects
of library service.

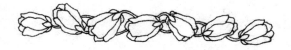

Right Speech

The best words in the best order.
—Samuel Taylor Coleridge,
Table Talk

The Buddha's instructions on leading a moral life were to purify the mind, to do good, and to avoid sin. "Sin" in this case is not concerned with breaking some divine law but with the aberrations and distortions of individual minds. Here again we see that the Buddhist disciplines are centered on the individual and his or her capacity for change, rather than on external forces and "higher powers." These "sins" include speaking or writing falsely or maliciously. Right speech consists of avoiding the confusions and evasions of day-to-day life in favor of speaking and writing clearly and to the point. Since one cannot speak or write clearly when expressing unformulated or unresolved thoughts, right speech has to be preceded by right-directed thought and concentration. Right speech also involves something that is harder than concentration and thinking clearly for most of us. That is, in contravention of natural human tendencies, we would refrain from speaking frivolously, gossiping, and unfair and condemnatory language. Again, most of us are not Saint Francis of Assisi and must be allowed our times of frivolity, unfairness, chatter, and insincerity. Our libraries are communities and such things exist in every known community. We would like to live by a version of the Golden Rule that states: "Speak as you would be spoken of," but we can seldom aspire to that perfection. What we can aspire to is clear, unambiguous, and salient writing and speaking based on concentrated thought and planning.

The library and its services suffer in the absence of clear writing and speaking. Staff cannot understand and apply ill-written policies, and users cannot understand and use services that are described in language that they cannot comprehend. Librarianship is no more burdened with jargon than any other profession, but it is indisputable that there is too much jargon in our professional literature and that we too often assume that our users are familiar with some of that jargon.

I will speak and write
as clearly as I can.

Right Action

*Our deeds determine us as much
as we determine our deeds.*
—George Eliot, *Adam Bede*

Right action is one of the components of the morality (*sila*) discipline of Buddhist thought and may be the one that is embraced, in theory, by all of us irrespective of our philosophy, religion, and social opinions. The trick, of course, is not in the idea that we should all do the right thing, but in determining what the right thing is. We are all guided in our professional lives by our own concepts of right and wrong and by our own values, but we can also find guidance in the library-related statements of others—in particular, for American librarians, the American Library Association's Code of Ethics. That code (adopted by the ALA Council in June 1995) offers another "eightfold path." It addresses the service ethic of librarianship, intellectual freedom, privacy, intellectual property, collegiality, integrity, tolerance, and the pursuit of excellence. It should be noted that other library professional associations have similar ethical statements. One of the distinguishing marks of a profession is that it has a code of values or ethics that its practitioners share and that guides the way they carry out their work. These codes of ethics and practice are endorsed by their professional organizations and embody a broad consensus shared by the members of the profession as to how their duties should be carried out. All such statements can give guidance. In addition, most libraries operate in a context (a college, community, school, corporation, association, or government)

that possesses its own values, rules, and code of ethics. There-fore, librarians wishing to do the right thing can call on the tri-partite support of their personal values and ethics, the ethical statements of their professional association, and the code of ethics of the community in which they work.

So far so good. Of course, life is never that neat and ac-tions take place in real life, not in the abstractions of ethical statements, no matter how worthy. What happens when one or two of the three value systems (personal, professional, and institutional) conflict with the other or others? What happens when a librarian is utterly committed to, say, intellectual freedom because of all three systems but does not know how to apply that commitment to a particular case? The point is that most of us know what right action is in general terms, but are conflicted over many specific actions. Few of us believe in censorship, and most of us believe in selecting the best mate-rials for our libraries. Is the line between censorship and selec-tivity always completely clear? The most rigorous ethicist (Buddhist or otherwise) will say that we are but human and all we can do is to strive for perfection while accepting our human imperfection.

I will seek to act
in accordance
with the highest
ethical values.

Right Livelihood

*Who is to do the pleasant and
clean work, and for what pay?*

—John Ruskin,
Sesame and Lilies

Right livelihood is the third of the three components of the
Buddhist discipline of moral conduct (*sila*). Followers are
urged to have occupations that display compassion and loving
friendship and to avoid work that is harmful to others—notably work that takes lives or involves magic and astrology. It
seems to me that library work falls very comfortably into the
right livelihood category. We work to help others, to better individual lives and society, and to preserve the human record
and make it available to all, and our working lives are animated by a sense of tolerance and service. We enhance lives
rather than destroying them, and the only magic in librarianship is found in children's story hours and in the secret recesses of the MARC record.

One of the great intangible benefits of library work is the
sense of self-worth that comes when we realize that, no
matter how humdrum the day or week, we are playing a part
in bringing the good things of life to everyone and improving
our communities, one life at a time. A library serving a community of any kind (a village, school, city, college or university, corporation, government) enriches that community,
which would be impoverished and weakened if that library
did not exist. Even library users do not always appreciate how
much effort goes into a well-run, service-oriented library.

Books do not select and catalogue themselves. Electronic resources must be chosen and the machines we need to gain access to them must be installed and maintained. Services must be staffed, budgets accounted for, buildings cleaned, and the technological infrastructure kept in tip-top order. At the most basic level, the library's doors must be opened on time and all areas of the library must be staffed and functioning when that happens. Libraries require a lot of hard and dedicated work on the part of many people, each contributing their best in the pursuit of their right livelihood and their service to individuals, communities, and society.

*I will do my best in all
my library work.*

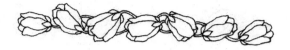

Right Effort

There is nothing that will not yield
to perseverance and method.
—Edmund Burke, *Letters*

Right effort is the first of the three parts of the "concentration" or "meditation" (*samadhi*) branch of the Buddhist Eightfold Path. Buddhist teaching stresses the need for effort—that is, for diligence, exertion, and unflagging perseverance. Effort is crucial because, in that philosophy, each person is charged with working out his or her own deliverance without reliance on external structures or forces. This doctrine of personal responsibility has similarities to the celebrated Protestant ethic in Western societies. My observation is that this ethic flourishes among those who work in libraries—Protestant, Buddhist, or of any other belief or nonbelief. The vast majority of librarians are characterized by hard work and the drive to get things accomplished. Who is more persevering than a reference librarian in hot pursuit of the elusive answer to a reference question?

However, perseverance, or what was called "stick-to-itiveness" in an earlier age, has its limits. There is always the question of how long anyone should persevere in what may seem a lost cause. We have always been told, "If at first you don't succeed, try, try again" (written by one W. E. Hickson in the nineteenth century), but W. C. Fields also had some sage advice: "If at first you don't succeed, try, try again. Then quit. No use being a damn fool about it." Two working days spent tracking down the cost of leather futures on the pre-World

War II Albanian stock exchange may be two days not spent on answering a score of less arcane but equally important questions. A perfectly catalogued book is a thing of beauty, but is it worth fifteen hours of delving into the uttermost recesses of MARC, *AACR2,* and the Library of Congress cataloguing rule interpretations? It all comes down to judgment and balance and the weighing of conflicting priorities. We must exert maximum effort in carrying out our service to individuals and society, but we must be judicious in deciding where, when, and for which purpose that effort is best exerted.

I will be diligent and
use that diligence wisely.

Proper Mindfulness

Give me, kind Heaven, a private station
A mind serene for contemplation.

—John Gay, *Fables*

Proper mindfulness is the second of the three parts of the "concentration" (*samadhi*) branch of the Buddhist Eightfold Path. The Buddha taught that his followers should train their minds to be free from confusion and disturbance, and that only by attaining this serenity could they reach higher levels of understanding. This proper mindfulness (an awareness of the higher things) makes those who possess it mentally strong, altruistic, broad-minded, tolerant, understanding, generous, and free from both illusions and delusions.

Could there be a better description of the ideal librarian? Surely every library user hopes that the library has collections assembled and catalogued by such people, and he or she would be a frequent user of a reference desk staffed by librarians with those mental attributes. Though few of us are bodhisattvas (those on the path to Buddhist perfection), we can aspire to such presence of mind and encourage ourselves and others to cultivate these excellent mental qualities. To put it another way, it is impossible to imagine an effective librarian who lacks all these mental qualities. Just to think of a narrow-minded, intolerant, selfish, and unsympathetic person plagued by illusions and delusions is to think of a kind of anti-librarian working in The Library from Hell. It is true that some librarians are occasionally intolerant or selfish, but it is also true that the overwhelming majority of librarians aspire to serve both

the individual users of their libraries and their community as a whole. Such service demands, at the very least, a measure of tolerance, inclusiveness, and selflessness and is impossible without those admirable qualities. Buddhists come to proper mindfulness through years of study and training, and it is unquestionably difficult for the rest of us to avoid the distractions and confusions engendered all the time by the press of work and the stresses of the modern world. However, it is not only good for us as librarians to work on attaining good mental qualities and rising above the distractions and confusions of daily life, it is also good for us as human beings seeking harmony and balance in all areas of our lives.

*I will aspire to be
broad-minded,
generous, and selfless
in my library work.*

Right Concentration

For there is a music wherever there is a harmony, order or proportion; and thusfar we may maintain the music of the spheres.

—Sir Thomas Browne,
Religio medici

Right concentration is the third of the three parts of the "concentration" (*samadhi*) branch of the Buddhist Eightfold Path and is the summation of the other seven factors of that path. Once he or she has achieved the other steps—right view, right speech, etc.—the successful traveler on the path achieves a state that is difficult to describe in English but is often characterized as one of equanimity.

> With the fading away as well of happiness he abides in equanimity, and, mindful and fully aware, still feeling pleasure with the body, he enters upon and abides in the third meditation, on account of which the noble ones announce: "He has a pleasant way of life and is an onlooker with equanimity and is mindful." (*Majjhima Nikaya,* or *Middle-Length Discourses of the Buddha*)

"Equanimity" is derived from two Latin words meaning "equality" and "mind" and is generally defined as an evenness of mental disposition and emotional balance, especially under stress. To the Buddhist, such an ideal state is only reached when the person rises above both pleasure and pain, is free from human suffering, and knows and sees everything.

This may seem far from the secular world of libraries and, indeed, from the real world of work that we all inhabit, but the

197

idea of balance and harmony and the idea of rising above the immediate concerns of the day are attractive in any setting. The great majority of us work and live in a stressful world of information overload, inadequate resources, underappreciation, and the constant strain of making do and doing more with less. These can take a toll on anyone and are hardly compatible with the harmonious life. Moreover, the idea of reducing stress and striving to achieve harmony and balance is as much medical as it is spiritual. I would argue that its medical benefits complement such benefits as improving the quality of work life and personal life. So, the question is not about the benefits of equanimity but about the means by which it is achieved. The Buddhist who has traveled so far will say that it is the result of years of training and meditation. The rest of us have to find another way. I believe that two ideas—concentration on our basic values and rising above the day-to-day concerns of work life—are central to harmony and balance in work life. These are simple ideas but not as easy as they may seem. However, if all our problems were measured against the basic ideas in which we believe—services, intellectual freedom, literacy, etc.—and if we can see the small irritations of work life as what they are—small and ultimately insignificant—then the search for harmony and balance will reach a successful conclusion.

I will seek harmony
in my library life.

The Golden Rule

Therefore all things whatsoever
ye would do that men should do to you,
do ye even so unto them.

—Matthew 7:12

Confucius (K'ung Fu Tzu, 551–479 BCE) is the best-known and most influential figure in the long history of China and its thought. A central Confucian concept is called *jen*—a state of perfection and virtue to which humans should aspire and to which all actions and thoughts should be directed. One aspect of *jen* is what is known in the West as the Golden Rule. One of the Four Books of Confucianism is called the *Analects,* in which we find a definition of a person of *jen*—"wishing to establish his own character, he also establishes the character of others; and wishing to be prominent himself, he also helps others to be prominent." Such a characterization shows how the ideal life is one that seeks balance between the needs and desires of the self and the imperatives of society and reaches the heights of altruism by always considering others. The words that we find in the Christian Gospels and Confucian writings also have their counterparts in Buddhist, Jewish, Muslim, Hindu, and Taoist writings as well as in those of other religions and of secular philosophers. They all express some version of "do as you would be done by"—the way in which humans are predisposed to the quest for harmony and balance and service to others, no matter how often and how far we fail in such noble aspirations. The *Tao-te Ching* of Lao Tzu (probably a near contemporary of Confucius) tells us that the wise person is

Kind to the kind
And is also kind to the unkind
For virtue is kind.
He is faithful to the faithful
He is also faithful to the unfaithful
For virtue is honest.

As it is in all other aspects of living in society, the Golden Rule is particularly applicable to librarianship. When we use a library, we expect to be greeted with civility and helpfulness; we expect equal access to recorded knowledge and information in all formats; we expect harmonious, welcoming, pleasant surroundings; and we expect to encounter up-to-date, comprehensive catalogues and informed, service-oriented reference librarians. These are the least we should expect and the least that others should expect of us. Putting yourself in the shoes of the library user (the good and the not so good, the virtuous and the not so virtuous) is always a salutary exercise, and following the Golden Rule is one of the very best ways of leading the library life.

**I will follow
the Golden Rule.**

Ten

This & That

Serendipity-doo-dah

*The princes were always making
discoveries, by accidents and sagacity,
of things they were not in quest of.*

—Horace Walpole,
on *The Three Princes of Serendip*

Bill Richardson is a gifted and witty Canadian broadcaster (and holder of an MLS degree) who hosts a show called *Bunny Watson* on Canadian Broadcasting Corporation radio. Those with a taste for library-themed movies will recognize the source of his title. Bunny Watson was the name of the character played by the immortal and indomitable Katharine Hepburn in *Desk Set* (1957). She is a librarian who stands up to the early information scientist Richard Sumner (Spencer Tracy), who proposes to replace Bunny Watson and her fellow librarians with a vast computer employing what look like Hollerith cards (in those far-off days punched cards had the same magical allure as computer disks do today). Bunny and the librarians triumph, naturally, and she comes to stand for the importance of the human mind and the skills of librarians when compared with the limitations of computers and the inhumanity of time-and-motion analysts like Tracy's character.

Although the struggle between librarians and those who would put them out of business continues nearly fifty years later and will continue as long as there are people who prize cost over value and machines over human values, that struggle is not the reason why Bill Richardson calls his show *Bunny Watson*. His theme is serendipity of the kind that librarians and

libraries make possible as no one and nothing else can. Libraries make possible connections between one book and another,
one website and another, between sound recordings, films,
pamphlets, reference sources, and the people they represent.
What is more powerful than a "see also" reference from a subject in which you are interested to another subject that you
have never thought about before? Bill Richardson and Bunny
Watson see the library as a complex net of interconnectedness
and know that all those interconnections are made possible by
the efforts of collection developers, cataloguers, reference librarians, and the rest. Sometimes a library use is simple. You
want something, go to the library to get it, and leave satisfied.
Sometimes it can be more than that. You look at a website on
a library computer and that reminds you of a book of which
you have not thought for years or takes you to an article by
someone completely unknown to you that, in turn, takes you
to a DVD of a half-forgotten movie. Once you have had that
experience, you understand the true glory of the library—that
complex and never-ending series of connections to the entire
human record.

I will relish
the discovery of things
that I was not seeking.

Bright, Shiny, and Evanescent

I'm forever blowing bubbles
Pretty bubbles in the air
They fly so high, nearly reach the sky
Then like my dreams they fade and die.

—Jaan Kenbrovin and
John William Kellette, 1919

I am an inveterate snipper of news stories and am always being taken by a story or idea and then squirreling a paper clipping away for future use (that use is all too often theoretical rather than actual). It was a natural progression from this lifelong habit to a new habit of saving the URLs of appealing websites into a "Favorites" or "Bookmarks" file. A quick look at, and random choice from, the long "Favorites" list on my home computer reveals sites on cricket, the Church of the Eternal Question, Calvin and Hobbes, the British comedians Dave Gorman (no relation) and Tony Hancock, and kaleidoscopes. Two problems come to mind. First, until looking at the list for this piece, I had completely forgotten all but those on cricket and Tony Hancock. Second, of the six sites, three are now unavailable at the URLs I have stored for them.

There is a particular resource that tends to contribute to my hoarding habit. The librarian and writer Marylaine Block publishes a terrific online service called "Neat New" (short for "Neat new stuff I found on the Web this week"), usually in tandem with her weekly thoughts on topics connected with all aspects of her career as an "itinerant Internet guru" and "librarian without walls" under the title "Ex Libris." Each week, Marylaine's subscribers are presented with a handful of web

goodies to marvel over and save for future reference. One recent issue contains a "site for daily updates, raw images, and videos of Saturn taken by the Cassini-Huygens spacecraft"; a "digital library of eighteenth, nineteenth and early twentieth century local and trade directories from England and Wales"; a site called "Making the Modern World," which tracks the inventions of the past century; a bimonthly magazine "for people who like to make stuff"; and the ever-popular site to find out "your risk for cancer, heart disease, diabetes, stroke, and osteoporosis, and how you could reduce those risks." Some of these are not very appealing to me (clues: I do not like reading about diseases or how to "make stuff"), but I think, if I save the others, I will use them one day! The sad fact is that if I ever do get around to using them, there is a high possibility that some of them will have faded and died. Bright shiny bubbles today—an error message and an unfindable or expired site tomorrow.

I will enjoy and use
electronic resources.

Blogs

I write for enjoyment and self-enlightenment.
—Sir Neville Cardus, *Conversations*

Neologisms are often unattractive, but even among them the word "blog" stands out for ugliness. It sounds like something you might find in a drain, but is in fact a contraction of "web log" and the name for unfiltered, unedited online musings and interpretations—sometimes by one person only and sometimes interactive. Each blog has a high quotient of narcissism, but then so had its pre-computer forerunner, the personal diary. Though the diaries of Samuel Pepys, Francis Kilvert, "An Edwardian Lady," and others were published to great acclaim and have been read with enjoyment by many, most personal diaries are of strictly limited appeal and that appeal is often limited to one person—the writer of the diary. When you look into the world of blogs, their antecedents in diaries rapidly become apparent. These accumulations of random observations and opinions almost invariably have a solipsistic air and very limited appeal. Each seems to have attractions only for a small number of people who contribute their own opinions and ideas to the blogger, who may then present them as received or weave them into her own writings. One difference between the personal diary of yore and the blog of today is that the authors of the latter appear to spend an inordinate amount of time on this activity, sometimes to the extent that the blog becomes the main focus of their lives. The "Globe of Blogs" website, which covers 13,000 blogs, posted a recommendation that its subscribers read Rhonda Van's first book, *The Bath Gourmet* (which tells you how to liven up a bath with the

addition of such ingredients as sesame oil, rosemary, and co-
conut milk), as "the perfect way to unwind after a brain-
twisting *day* [my emphasis] in front of the computer." They
also mention the "blogathon," an opportunity to write blogs
for twenty-four hours straight. The result of all this strenuous
activity is mind-numbing. Would the following have ever
been published in print?

> The weblog for pro wrestler/writer/EMT and general jack of
> all trades **** ***** who hails from Prospect, Oregon. Lots of
> discussion about my life, lots of idiot bashing, lots of pro-
> wres [sic] discussion, lots of ranting, and I'll even mix in a
> little of everything else.

Then there is the blog that consists of "Thoughts and essays about music, physics, martinis and pretty girls." Works of
genius have been written about far less promising topics than
wrestling and pretty girls, and most first novels, even some of
the best, are essentially about their authors and very little else.
Unfortunately, if there are writers of genius, or talent, or even
basic competence out there blogging, I have yet to find them.
In the early heady days of the Internet, we were promised
that, in the future, everyone could be published. Alas, that
promise is being fulfilled, which should remind us all to be
wary of what we wish for.

I will seek and read
the enlightening
and the creative.

Beyond the Boundaries

*When they study our civilization two
thousand years from now, there will be three
things that Americans will be known for:
the Constitution, baseball, and jazz music.
They're the three most beautiful things
Americans have ever created.*

—Gerald Early, in Ken
Burns's *Baseball*, 1994

The three quintessential American creations cited by Gerald
Early have something else in common. They each start from a
set of rules and then go on with infinite variations. Baseball
games have no fixed duration and contain within them a be-
wildering array of plays, stratagems, and substitutions so that
no game is exactly like any other. Jazz musicians start with a
tune and take it to wherever their fancy directs them for as
long as they wish. Improvisation is at the heart of their art. The
U.S. Constitution contains a set number of articles and a po-
tentially limitless number of amendments. Moreover, apart
from the few who regard its eighteenth-century wording as in-
errant and incapable of interpretation, the general consensus
and practice are that it is the job of legislators and the judiciary
to interpret the Constitution in the light of modern circumstances. In each case, it is the job of the principal agents (baseball players, musicians, and lawyers) to find a multiplicity of
variations on the basic themes.

I do not think it far-fetched to think about librarianship in
these terms. We too have basic rules and basic values, and it is

the job of all of us to interpret those rules and values in the light of the mission of each library and the circumstances in which we find ourselves. Nothing is more rule-driven than cataloguing, but cataloguers are putting a lot of effort into applying those rules to the freakishness of electronic documents and to the creation of global electronic catalogues. The values of service and stewardship are alive and well and they are being applied in areas such as virtual reference and the preservation of web documents. The "library as place" is just as important today as it was a century ago, but librarians are adapting to new kinds of library buildings and new services that reach out beyond those buildings. Just as jazz, baseball, and the Constitution remain recognizable no matter how great the adaptations and how numerous the changes, librarianship too remains recognizable even as it adapts to the changed circumstances of the twenty-first century.

*I will approach
my profession
with flexibility and
open-mindedness.*

Singing the Library

Love in the library
Quiet and cool
Love in the library
There are no rules
Surrounded by stories
Surreal and sublime
I fell in love in the library.
                    —Jimmy Buffett

What do Manic Street Preachers, Grrrrls, Boyzvoice, Railroad Jerk, Shriekback, and M. C. Poindexter & the Study Crew have in common? (Apart from the fact that I had never heard of any of them before today, that is. I am sure that you, gentle reader, are more au courant.) They have all written or recorded songs about or set in libraries.* I have heard of and cherished Jimmy Buffett for decades but was unaware that his interests went beyond parrots, pirates, margaritas, sailing, the Keys, coral reefs and Coral Reefers, and Hawaiian shirts to discovering romance in libraries and their users. What could be more poignant than his lyrics "Past the newspaper racks on the worn marble floor / Near Civil War History my heart skipped a beat / She was standing in Fiction stretched high on bare feet"? Perhaps her sending him "a smile as she reached for Flaubert."

Parrothead Jimmy is not alone among songsters in finding romance. Railroad Jerk sang "Sweeeet librarian /

* I am indebted to Fiona Bradley, a librarian in Sydney, Australia, and her website "Blisspix" (the "Bliss" part refers both to the state and to the faceted Bliss classification scheme) for the information about library songs.

What good books can you recommend?" on their 1996 album *The Third Rail*—perhaps the only reference to the readers' advisory function in the annals of popular song. Piano Magic (a radiophonic band) take an odd view of the duties of a librarian in their song "I Am the Sub-Librarian." The unfortunate woman suffers from "Paranormal ill-health from dusting off the top shelf" and, the song tells us, is variously a counter girl, a tea maker, a swan feeder, and a spectacle breaker. I have certainly given library service from behind a counter in my time, have made tea for colleagues, and have broken (my own) spectacles in the line of duty. I feel that my library life has a serious deficiency in that I have never been associated with a library that had any swans and certainly have never fed any. Sam Phillips's lyrics for his "To the Library" as performed by the neo-punk band Faster Pussycat also break new ground— library use as innuendo. The writer offers to "open every book to you / tricks you've never learned / I'll take you to a place / we'll go where the action is / if you don't know what to do / I'll look it up for you." Lux Occulta, a heavy metal Goth band to judge from their publicity, have a suitably doom-laden song called "Library on Fire" in which they refer to librarians, asking "How safe do you feel hidden behind letters, ciphers, numbers, names?" As far as this lapsed cataloguer is concerned, the answer is "not very," especially as the song closes with "I set the Library ablaze / I kiss the curse of wisdom goodbye." There is some solace, though, in Shriekback's "Lines from the Library," which contains the oddly comforting "I've heard say: / The printed word and the paper it's printed on / Not worth anythin'. . . . If it's good enough for Geoffrey Chaucer / It's OK by me too." I'm with Shriekback and Geoffrey Chaucer.

I will look at libraries from all angles.

Rocks of Ages

*Science is nothing but trained
and organized common sense.*

—T. H. Huxley,
The Method of Zadig

On March 7, 1785, a man little known to history, the Scot James Hutton, changed our view of the world forever. Until his paper (delivered on that day to the Royal Society of Edinburgh for the reticent Hutton by his friend, the chemist Joseph Black), it was established wisdom that the entire world began in 4004 BCE. The latter "fact" was computed by the Irish archbishop James Ussher from a careful reading of the Old Testament. Though *books* can enhance our understanding of the world and lead to the creation of new knowledge, it is apparent from the evidence of history that reliance on a literal reading of one book can lead away from the light of knowledge. Even in the twenty-first century, there are those who rely on a single religious text for their understanding of the material world, society, and all things secular or not, as well as their spiritual, moral, and religious life.

Hutton found Ussher's biblically derived chronology incredible in the light of his painstaking and comprehensive study of rocks, outcroppings, and geological strata in Scotland and England. Those studies convinced him that the Earth was far older than scripture or eighteenth-century science could measure. In fact, his theory was that the world was in a constant state of decay and renewal, of continuous cycles of shifting rock visible in the geologic record. Moreover, in his view, that cyclical process had neither a beginning nor an end.

Both the religious and the scientific establishments of the age heavily criticized him. Though few now believe in a universe, solar system, and planet Earth without a beginning or an end, the essential truth of what Hutton saw in the rocks is now received wisdom. We now believe in the Big Bang (in the words of the philosopher Dave Barry, we believe that in the beginning there was nothing and then it exploded) and know that the Sun is a minor star and the Earth a planet both with a fixed origin and a certain end. However, it cannot be doubted that James Hutton is part of modern science, in at the very beginning of the separation of scientific inquiry from religious belief that is at the heart of modern Western society. He found truth in the rocks of Britain in the same way that we can find truth in the books preserved and made accessible by libraries, if we take the time to read widely with skeptical, inquiring eyes.

I will read widely
and seek understanding.

The People's Information

Who controls the past controls the future.
Who controls the present controls the past.
—George Orwell, 1984

Every now and then, and increasingly since 2001, the federal government has asked government documents depository libraries to return or destroy documents in various formats that have been deposited in those libraries. The request to return or destroy is often stated to be at the request of the Department of Homeland Security (CD-ROMs containing information about national parks and other nationally owned resources, for example) or the Department of Justice (documents relating to various statutes concerning the federal seizure of the assets of criminals and money launderers, for example). The idea is that there is a class of government information that can be misused by terrorists and criminals and, therefore, must be removed from any possible scrutiny by malefactors and, as a consequence, from the rest of us. A recent memorandum from the superintendent of documents said: "Please withdraw these materials immediately and destroy them by any means to prevent disclosure of their contents." *By any means?* Bonfires, anyone?

Many things come to mind in contemplating this state of affairs, but two of them seem to be urgently important. The first is a notion in which most of us believe instinctively—that information and recorded knowledge, once launched into the world, must be cherished, preserved, and transmitted to posterity. Almost anyone living in a democratic society recoils

from the idea of things being removed from the human record. We look at book burning in Nazi Germany, the purging of libraries (and librarians) in Stalin's Soviet Union, and the destruction of texts, sound recordings, and images in a variety of lesser tyrannies, including local governments within Western democracies. This kind of thing should be abhorrent to all of us. Our library shelves are full of books and other materials that can be used in a criminal manner or of which the government of the day might disapprove. Once we accept the idea that there are people in government who can say what is or is not suitable to be in our collections, what is to prevent them from demanding the removal of non-governmental materials from our library collections?

The second issue is the question of the best way to issue government recorded knowledge and information. At first blush, it seemed like a good idea to transfer government information to digital form and make the resources for which we as taxpayers have paid (let it never be forgotten—it is *our* information, we own it) available quickly to all. But there are two problems. First, not everyone has access to or familiarity with computers, and when they do, they may not have the resources to print many pages of government information in which they might be interested. Second, the model proposed by the federal government is of central databases to which libraries will be allowed access. The documents will not be distributed electronically to reside in local databases, in the way that paper documents are distributed to reside in local libraries. The government will control the databases and the documents that it wishes to censor and delete. In that future, the superintendent of documents (if such a person exists) need

not trouble to issue instructions to return or destroy; the Justice Department or some other agency will simply remove what it does not like from the database and no one will be any the wiser. In fact, we will all be dumber.

I will work to preserve
free access for all
to government information.

Music Librarians

Music, the greatest good that mortals know
And all of heaven we have below.

—Joseph Addison,
A Song for St. Cecilia's Day

An essay in a recent book on music librarianship states that the necessary preconditions for success in music librarianship are, in addition to professional training, a love of music and a service ethic. It would have been quite common, 100 years ago, to read that a librarian should have a love of reading and a commitment to service, but this is rare now that many of us are no longer people of the book. Music librarians see themselves as special; members of the library profession but on a slightly higher plane. That self-assessment depends, I suspect, on precisely the requirement of loving music—the fact that success in their jobs centers on a love of and knowledge of a particular form of human expression. Do documents librarians love government documents, and have those been part of their lives since they were children? Do rare book librarians spend their weekends reading incunabula or unraveling mysteries of historical bibliography? Do systems librarians enjoy an evening in front of the fire reading Windows manuals? (Well, perhaps some do, but that is another story.) Children's librarians love children's literature, but one suspects they love service to children and the awakening of their minds and uplifting of their hearts more. Also, after a hard day in the children's library, they probably relax with Mozart and detective novels or hip-hop music and Dickens or television shows not intended

for children. In contrast, most music librarians I have known relax by listening to music, or by playing music or singing in addition to the recreations of the rest of us. In short, music librarians live all aspects of their lives with a musical accompaniment; their private and working lives are marinated in music, and that is what makes them different from us.

A hundred years ago, a librarian could spend her or his working day immersed in literature, doing readers' advisory work, becoming acquainted with the content of collections, and generally leading a sort of literary life at work and at home. We are far more likely to encounter an Elvis impersonator than a literary lady or gentleman in today's libraries, but the musical music librarian is among us in great numbers. The other special thing about music librarianship is that technology is furthering their musicality by offering more and more ways of listening to, collecting, and preserving music. Technology has had some baleful effects on literature and reading (and some fewer beneficial effects), but its impact on the world of music and the librarians who are, by definition, part of that world, seems to have been uniformly positive.

> *I will appreciate*
> *the contributions*
> *music librarians make*
> *to our profession.*

Hispanic, Latino, Chicano?

A knowledge of one other culture should
sharpen our ability to scrutinize more carefully,
to appreciate more lovingly, our own.
—Margaret Mead, *Coming of Age in Samoa*

Of all the human categories invented by modern society, that of "Hispanic" is one of the most amorphous and elusive. It derives from Hispania—the ancient Roman name for the Iberian Peninsula—and, strictly speaking, refers to anyone of Spanish or Portuguese descent. In the United States today, the term is used for all persons of Spanish-language heritage whether they speak Spanish, Spanish and English, or only English. It also applies to those from an area with a Spanish-language heritage—for example, to a Mexican who speaks a Native American language only. It is, therefore, not a linguistic categorization and certainly not an ethnic or racial classification—Hispanics can be of African, European, or Native American heritage. Spanish was the first non-indigenous language to be spoken widely in the Americas, and Spanish speakers have lived in large areas of the American West for centuries, under Spanish and later U.S. rule. In the words of a Tejano saying, "We never crossed the border, the border crossed us." The popular view of Hispanics as newcomers and even intruders could not be further from the truth.

From the library point of view, there are two overlapping issues to be faced: the first is service to those whose only or

primary language is Spanish, and the second is service to areas in which one of the Hispanic cultures is predominant. The language issue is complicated by the fact that Spanish takes many forms in different parts of the huge Spanish-speaking world. Hispanics in the United States have their origins (in descending order of the largest populations) in Mexico; the Dominican Republic and Central and South America; Puerto Rico; and Cuba. Each group speaks different versions of Spanish, each of which is influenced, particularly among the young, by interaction with English speakers. Though there are cultural similarities between all Hispanic groups, the culture and needs of Hispanic communities will vary from one group to another. A library in a Dominican area of New York City will face some different challenges from those of a library in a predominantly Mexican (Chicano) town in California's Central Valley.

There are, of course, far too many aspects of library service to this increasingly large and important group in U.S. society to be dealt with this briefly, but there are some general principles that can be listed. Knowledge of, and sensitivity to, the culture and language are essential, as is a recognition that Hispanics are far from a monolithic group. Help in negotiating an English-speaking official world is vital if a library is to serve those who are predominantly Spanish speaking. Collections must reflect the interests and needs of the community and should provide reading and viewing that are both expected and challenging. In particular, the needs of children and young adults with one foot in the Hispanic world and one foot in the Anglo world can only be met by library services that demonstrate an understanding of the complexity of their lives. It is

not the job of the library to transform society, but in this case
as in many others, the library exists in a society in which the
past, present, and future intermingle, and it can assist any and
all in dealing with that complexity.

I will embrace
the diversity
of library users.

Retirement

Each of us is acutely conscious of our own self. We are aware, but less intensely aware, of the selves of those we love; even less intensely aware of acquaintances, colleagues who are not so close, and distant relatives; hardly aware of the selves of the thousands of people we encounter in the course of years; and not aware at all of the individuality of those we have never met. That is why the statement "Tens of thousands die in Bangladesh" resonates, for all but a few, far less than an individual family tragedy. These expanding ripples of increasing indifference can only be overcome by great literature, music, and art, because only they make us aware of the lives of the unknown and far away. The reason why the great changes in life—leaving home, first job, marriage, moving, divorce, bereavement, etc.—have such a profound effect on us is that they, each in their own way, disrupt our own self-awareness and also change our consciousness of the selves of others by introducing new selves and removing others.

Retirement, an increasing preoccupation of many librarians, is such a life-changing event. Rock 'n' rollers never retire, nor do most writers, actors, moviemakers, painters, and others in the arts. Lawyers and doctors retire every day, unless they are Supreme Court justices or internationally famous heart surgeons. I know a number of librarians who are working past

the usual retirement age, even though their pension situation is such that they work, essentially, for nothing or even at a loss. These are the people who center their life on their work, not because their lives are otherwise empty or because work is a cure for what ails them, but because they are devoted to the ideals behind what they do and to the mission of the libraries in which they work. We may not be artists or rockers, but neither are we wage slaves or drudges. Librarianship is a means of keeping the wolf from the door (if not an especially lucrative means), but it is far more than that. It is a calling and a vocation that has ideals, values, and rewards that never trouble the IRS. Small wonder that it is often difficult for librarians to walk away at the end of their careers and separate themselves from the environment in which they have worked.

Those of us who are approaching retirement have many models: those who continue to work; those who leave but remain in touch with their libraries, colleagues, and professional associations; those who separate themselves from their libraries but remain professionally active; and those who pack up and then sail, fly, or take the train to dream houses on the beach, in the mountains, in far-off countries or on the other side of town and leave their jobs, colleagues, and profession behind. There is nothing wrong with any of these choices, and there is everything right about a working library life spent in services to individuals and society.

*I will cherish my work in libraries
and enjoy my life after it.*

Michael Gorman is dean of library services at the Henry Madden Library, California State University, Fresno. He was the first editor of the *Anglo-American Cataloguing Rules,* Second Edition (1978) and of the 1988 revision of that work. He is the author of a number of books, including *Our Enduring Values* (2000), the winner of the ALA's Highsmith Award in 2001 for the best book on librarianship. Gorman has been the recipient of numerous awards, including the Margaret Mann Citation in 1979 and the Melvil Dewey Medal in 1992. He was elected vice-president and president-elect of the American Library Association in 2004.